# Praise for *The Definitive Guide to Social CRM*

"Barton Goldenberg's *The Definitive Guide to Social CRM* is just that: a clear and detailed step-by-step outline for embracing social CRM organization-wide, complete with his proven methodologies for strategy and technology adoption within a business. It's just the primer needed to help business leaders outline how to approach social CRM in their enterprise."
—**Ginger Conlon**, Editor-in-Chief, *Direct Marketing News*

---

"Barton Goldenberg has been at the forefront of Customer Relationship Management for 30 years. As a regular columnist to *CRM Magazine* since our launch in 1997, Barton has influenced our audience in print, online, and as a conference chair and speaker at our annual CRM Evolution Conference & Exhibition. Barton has also written extensively for many other media outlets and has been a highly sought after speaker at numerous industry events. Social CRM is still in its early stages of development and Barton's newest book, *The Definitive Guide to Social CRM* is a must read for anyone trying to get verifiable return-on-investment with their Social CRM projects."
—**Bob Fernekees**, VP/Group Publisher, CRM Media, a division of Information Today, Inc.

---

"While Pyrotek is just now dipping our toe in the social media waters, we feel very fortunate to have Barton—and his new book—as our guide while we begin forming a Social CRM strategy."
—**Joe Tarulli**, Corporate Sales Development Manager, Pyrotek Inc.

---

"Social CRM is critical to customer engagement in today's social media driven world. Barton brings his 30 years of experience with helping best-in-class companies with their customer-centric initiatives to bear in this timely analysis of how to do Social CRM right."
—**Mike Merriman**, Vice President, Sales & Marketing, Mzinga

---

"As an ISM client, we know the experience and expertise Barton brings to customer-centric initiatives. In his new book, Barton shares his expertise with case studies and a clearly defined roadmap for Social CRM adoption."
—**Chip Devine**, Vice President–MultiChannel Business, Ferguson

---

"Social CRM is the next wave that will engage an organization's customer relationship efforts through an interplay of Social Media with CRM. As Social CRM is forecasted to grow to a $9 billion global market by 2018, this book will teach the reader how to benefit from this growing phenomenon.

"No matter the business—or the customer—knowing your customers is key. That's why Social CRM and Barton's definitive book are so important."
—**Ron Klyn**, Chief Information Officer, Universal Forest Products Inc.

---

"From shaping CRM to understanding today's omni-channel digital customer, Barton Goldenberg leads the way again with his compelling insights and methodologies. The timing of his latest book, *The Definitive Guide to Social CRM*, once again demonstrates his forward thinking."
—**Bob Dunfee**, 25-Year CRM Veteran

---

"From shaping CRM to understanding today's digital client, Barton Goldenberg stays ahead of the curve. That's why his book on incorporating Social CRM into your customer-centric strategies is so important and timely."
—**Tim Bajarin**, President, Creative Strategies

---

"Barton Goldenberg and his team at ISM have already demonstrated Social CRM success with clients such as AAA, Marriott, ExxonMobil, and Kraft Foods, so when creating your Social CRM roadmap, you'll absolutely want to read *The Definitive Guide to Social CRM*."
—**Bob McLaughlin**, Former Sr. VP, McGraw-Hill

---

"Barton Goldenberg is simply the most effective transformational leader I have met. His business acumen is matched only by his ability to understand the dimensions behind how change stems from a customer's needs to a firm's operations. Now Barton in his new book, *The Definitive Guide to Social CRM*, captures how a firm should plan, manage, and leverage social media as a means to increase the bottom line. What makes this book so insightful is the integration of social media capabilities with those of CRM; the narrative is both compelling and practical for any leader trying to bring customer relationship capabilities to fruition—the narrative is a roadmap on how to make that outcome a reality."
—**Cyrus Aram,** Senior Director, Blue Shield of California and Lecturer, University of California, Davis

---

"The one book executives of companies competing for today's digital customer should read is *The Definitive Guide to Social CRM*."
—**Neal Keene**, VP of Indirect Sales/Customer Engagement Solutions, Pitney Bowes

# The Definitive Guide to Social CRM

Maximizing Customer Relationships with Social Media to Gain Market Insights, Customers, and Profits

Barton J. Goldenberg
Founder and President, ISM, Inc.

Publisher: Paul Boger
Editor-in-Chief: Amy Neidlinger
Executive Editor: Jeanne Glasser Levine
Operations Specialist: Jodi Kemper
Cover Designer: Alan Clements
Managing Editor: Kristy Hart
Project Editor: Elaine Wiley
Copy Editor: Bart Reed
Proofreader: Jess DeGabriele
Senior Indexer: Cheryl Lenser
Compositor: Nonie Ratcliff
Manufacturing Buyer: Dan Uhrig

© 2015 by Barton J. Goldenberg

Upper Saddle River, New Jersey 07458

For information about buying this title in bulk quantities, or for special sales opportunities (which may include electronic versions; custom cover designs; and content particular to your business, training goals, marketing focus, or branding interests), please contact our corporate sales department at corpsales@pearsoned.com or (800) 382-3419.

For government sales inquiries, please contact governmentsales@pearsoned.com.

For questions about sales outside the U.S., please contact international@pearsoned.com.

Company and product names mentioned herein are the trademarks or registered trademarks of their respective owners.

Printed in the United States of America
First Printing March 2015

ISBN-10: 0-13-413390-0
ISBN-13: 978-0-13-413390-4

Pearson Education LTD.
Pearson Education Australia PTY, Limited.
Pearson Education Singapore, Pte. Ltd.
Pearson Education Asia, Ltd.
Pearson Education Canada, Ltd.
Pearson Educación de Mexico, S.A. de C.V.
Pearson Education—Japan
Pearson Education Malaysia, Pte. Ltd.

Library of Congress Control Number: 2014959167

The Definitive Guide to Social CRM *is dedicated*
*to my professional colleagues and friends*
*in the CRM industry. For 30 years your guidance*
*and support have been invaluable,*
*and I extend a hearty thanks to you all.*

# Contents

# About the Author

**Barton Goldenberg**, Founder & President of ISM, Inc.
*Leading customer-centric strategist, author, speaker, and futurist*

For 30 years Barton Goldenberg, ISM, Inc.'s founder and president, has challenged executive audiences on the topic of customer-centric business strategies. He designs and delivers insightful, entertaining, and informative presentations that incorporate live case studies taken from ISM's best-in-class clients.

Barton has always occupied a leading role in providing a lifecycle approach to customer relationships, from founding a pioneering firm in 1985, when the concept of customer relationship management (CRM) was taking form, to being one of the first three inductees into the CRM Hall of Fame.

## Customer-Centric Presentations

Barton frames his customer-centric business strategy presentations within the people/process/technology paradigm, and references a variety of tools and techniques in support of these strategies, including CRM/ Social CRM, Big Data analytics and insight, knowledge communities, customer experience, and channel optimization. Barton's results-oriented, bottom-line presentations have been praised by audiences worldwide, including clients such as AAA, Delta Faucet, Deutsche Bank, Exxon-Mobil, Ferguson, Giorgio Armani, IBM, Jaguar Land Rover, Johnson Controls, Kraft Foods, Marriott, McGraw-Hill, Merck, Pfizer, Roche, Schlumberger, T. Rowe Price, Zumba Fitness, and more.

## Meeting Customer Expectations in Real Time

For today's always-on, always-connected consumer, collaboration is the key in the customer lifecycle. Whether business-to-business or business-to-consumer, customer expectations must be met in real time, which Barton addresses in his book, *CRM in Real Time: Empowering Customer Relationships*, published by Information Today. His earlier book, *CRM Automation* (Prentice Hall), is considered the primer for companies implementing customer-focused programs. ISM's Software Lab publishes the benchmark *Guide to Mobile & Social CRM Automation* (now in its 20th edition). Barton is a columnist for *CRM Magazine* and is often quoted in business and trade publications.

Prior to founding ISM, Barton held senior management positions at the U.S. Department of State and Monsanto Europe S.A. He holds a B.S. (Economics) with honors from the Wharton School of Business and an M.S. (Economics) from the London School of Economics. Presently, Barton serves as the area governor for Rotary District 7620, after serving in 2013–2014 as president of the metroBethesda Rotary Club.

# Introduction

For the past 30 years I have had the honor of participating in the CRM industry. During that time it has been my pleasure to work with the world's biggest and best corporations on their CRM efforts (visit www.ismguide.com for a client list). I have chaired dozens of industry conferences, made hundreds of keynotes, and have written many columns and articles for numerous magazines. However, nothing has given me as much gratification as publishing industry-related books. My first book, *CRM Automation*, was published in 2003; the second, *CRM in Real Time*, was published in 2008. Both of them forecasted the next waves in CRM.

My new book, *The Definitive Guide to Social CRM*, focuses on the third wave in CRM: the integration of Social Media and CRM. This wave has already begun to change the nature of the industry, and it will continue to do so over the next five to ten years. Because of Social Media's phenomenal growth, we are now able to listen to, harvest, and integrate insights and customer information from social sites into your organization's CRM application to use in customer engagement activities.

I hope you enjoy *The Definitive Guide to Social CRM* and that you will contact me with your own thoughts and ideas. CRM is our industry to grow, and you can have a role in helping Social CRM blossom.

Barton Goldenberg
Bethesda, Maryland
February 2015

# Part I
# The Impact of Social Media on Customer Relationships

# 1

## Social CRM: The Intersection of Social Media and CRM

For decades organizations have had one-way conversations with their customers where the organizations did all the talking. Now, with the advent of Social Media, organizations and customers engage in two-way dialogues. This has transformed the rules of the marketplace.

Social Media is the newest way for organizations to communicate with and relate to employees, consumers, partners, and other stakeholders. It is enabling customers to have their say by posting exactly what they think about any organization's products, services, and policies—for everyone to see. Social Media is all about the ability of individuals to connect and share freely online through a set of highly interactive technology tools that leverage the fundamental human desire to interact with others. A major result of its growing influence has been to foster a shift in thinking away from promoting an organization's wares to seeking new ways to interact with customers to provide value. The more perceived value an organization can provide, the better its relationships will be with customers, thus improving loyalty and growing revenue. Social Media and its integration with CRM drive home the concept of customer-centric services, so that organizations can grow from closing sales to deepening long-term customer relationships and driving customer advocacy. Using Social CRM, organizations worldwide are maximizing customer relationships via Social Media to gain customers, market insights, and profits.

Social Media has been having such a strong influence on businesses worldwide, and even the experts cannot clearly visualize the total impact it will have. What is clear is that organizations that do not embrace Social Media will be sidelined in the near term, and possibly left behind in the marketplace of the future. Pew Internet.org's "Social Media Update 2013" found that 73 percent of U.S. online adults are using a social-networking platform such as Facebook, LinkedIn, or Twitter. The average American worker currently spends 1.2 hours a day on Social Media–related tasks, and 61 percent of online Americans under 30 use Social Media–related websites daily. Organizations of all kinds are being forced to make sense of this new channel for consumer interaction as this chorus of conversations and the proliferation of technologies that enable participation in Social Media grow.

Social Media is forcing organizations to find a definitively more customer-centered focus because it stimulates interaction between organizations and customers. Organizations must learn new ways to communicate effectively in this arena. How companies choose to adapt to this two-way dialogue environment will have an enormous impact on many organizations' sustainability. When an organization invests in a Social Media presence, customers are more likely to respond and join in on conversations. Customers really appreciate when a business reaches out to them (instead of the other way around) as well as when they are able to create a dialogue with a business. In many organizations, Social Media can be used to go that extra mile for customers, helping to separate the organizations from competing providers.

Organizations willing to explore and embrace this new business world order learn how to minimize the impact of negative posts on Social Media communities. Negative customer comments in Social Media communities can damage an organization's reputation, making access to all Social Media–related resources used to track and monitor Social Media activity vital for quickly and efficiently engaging customers and resolving disputes. This, in turn, can also improve an organization's image in the eyes of others who read Social Media posts. In addition, positive experiences that customers share can also be openly viewed on Social Media communities. This type of feedback often vastly outweighs positive statements made by the organization about its products and services in traditional marketing venues such as advertising, and is worth more than the expensive ad campaigns needed to attract new customers.

Customer relationship management (CRM) is a business approach that integrates *people, process,* and *technology* to maximize relationships with all customers, providing seamless collaboration between all customer-facing functions. It increasingly leverages the Internet and Social Media. Social CRM is the next logical step in CRM's evolution, and was forecast by MarketsandMarkets in a May 2013 study to grow to a $9-billion-plus worldwide market by the end of 2018.

Social CRM offers organizations the ability to harvest information from Social Media communities, integrate this information into customer profiles, and use the expanded profile to better personalize customer service, marketing messages, and sales offers. Using Social CRM, an organization can gather data about customers from information they have placed online, such as their opinions on a product or service, by using Social Media tools. Afterward, filtered customer information can be placed into an organization's Social CRM system and added to the appropriate customer profile. The organization can then use this information to personalize its customer communications so that customers will receive only organizational communications relevant to them. Although understanding what is relevant to an organization's customers can be a real challenge, a company's staff can use various Social Media analytics tools, online surveys, and polls, as well as relevant comments that customers post on various social communities.

At present, most organizations are just gathering *transactional* information concerning customers or prospects (that is, what they have purchased, when, and at what price), along with basic demographic information, including where the customer lives, works, job title, and so on, and placing this information in their Social CRM system. Using Social Media, an organization can now easily gather additional information, called *sentiment,* from customers, including their attitudes, likes and dislikes, and sentiments on various topics and issues that impact the organization. Furthermore, with Social Media, an organization's staff can easily open a two-way, online conversation with their customers and prospects relating to their preferences and their emotional content concerning the organization's products and services.

The most successful product offers are those that are most relevant to the target customer. An organization can determine product-offer relevancy from Social Media postings by gathering and analyzing customers' and prospects' attitudes, preferences, thoughts, and reviews. An organization can also find out what people are most interested in, what they care about, what their buying history and so on is, and obtain customer and prospect feedback about certain products and services. Social Media can also help companies acquire sentiment analysis from customers and prospects and then incorporate it in a way that will be communicated to the organizations' constituencies. Social CRM enables organizations to harvest such information and use it to make customer communications and product or service offerings that, as a result, are more appropriate and more relevant to their target audiences. This functionality has never been available before.

## How Social CRM Engages the Customer

The benefits of Social CRM are many, as exemplified in this list of what Social CRM can bring towards customer engagement for an organization:

- Captures indirect feedback from customers on social networks and communities that adds insight into the emotional side of the relationship
- Shares ideas for innovation by leveraging customer insights that can result in co-development of new products and services
- Enables customers to get help from other customers by decreasing service costs
- Generates brand awareness and visibility
- Increases web traffic and advertising income
- Assists in sales, marketing, and service efforts by sharing contacts in a sales community, marketing trends in a marketing community, and service issues in a service community

The impact of Social CRM is expected to be tremendous in the next few years. In a February 2011 Digital Marketing report, Gartner stated that social marketing processes will influence at least 80 percent of consumers' discretionary spending by the end of 2015. Gartner also stated in its 2014 "Magic Quadrant for the CRM Customer Engagement Center" report that 50 percent of its clients were using some type of Social Media applications within their Social CRM systems at the end of 2013. Social CRM has the potential to bring new and dynamic methods for improving customer service to organizations. It is also creating opportunities for new and existing providers in the customer service and contact center infrastructure markets. Current Social CRM vendors have typically come from two directions—the traditional CRM market, in which vendors are adding Social CRM capabilities, and from Social Media platform startup suppliers, which are focused on customer engagement. Social CRM is in its infancy, appearing in a fully realized form in only a limited number of businesses so far; yet, major organizations already are clamoring to harness the tremendous potential of Social CRM functionality.

# Social CRM Benefits

Key benefits resulting from Social CRM include the following:

- **Sales staff** can access significantly more relevant information about their customers and prospects from an integrated view of their Social Media activities using digital analytics (website visits, Internet searches, mobile activities, email, and so on) and existing Social CRM activity history.

- **Marketing staff** can meet prospects at their point of need, connecting much earlier in the buying process by leveraging real-time listening and monitoring of Social Media activities. Marketers can also gain a greater insight into the effectiveness of their marketing and communication efforts to their customers and prospects. In addition, they can compare which types of Social Media forums and communities are most effective in generating positive word of mouth, resulting in desired actions on an organization's website or on other digital channels. Afterward, the marketing staff can calculate the ROI of their content marketing and outreach efforts by connecting associated Social Media activities to website traffic, downloads, sales, or other desired actions.

- **Product development staff** can engage and collaborate directly with customers and prospects throughout the development phases, from the initial generation of ideas (known as *ideation*) through the phases of design, prototyping, and testing new or modified products and services, which can drive down costs and deliver significant advocacy and positive marketplace word of mouth.

- **Customer service staff** can provide memorable service by proactively responding to customers with an integrated view of their entire interaction, engagement, and Social Media activity history.

- **Community and Social Media staff** can access the Social Media content generated by customers and prospects for use on their outreach and engagement efforts.

# Social Media Has Taken Off in the Current Marketplace

The tremendous growth of three Social Media websites—Facebook, LinkedIn, and Twitter—has made these sites as familiar to many people as is Google. In addition to Social Media websites, blogs also play a key role in the evolution of Social Media. Facebook, LinkedIn, and Twitter have become so popular that marketers now have studies to show which online community to use to reach customers and prospects in specific industries, including advertising, agriculture, airlines, banking, biotechnology, health care, manufacturing, pharmaceutical, real estate, and more.

## More and More People Are Using Social Media

The time and money being spent on Social Media is astounding, as indicated by the following Social Media statistics:

- In 2013, 1.7 billion people were online (ISM research).
- Community members spend 54 percent more than nonmembers (eBay).
- Members spend 50 percent longer in social communities than non-community users (Forum One Networks).
- Live support costs $12 per call, versus $.25 for online self-service (Forrester).
- Approximately 56 percent of online community members log on once a day or more (Center for Digital Future).
- Members visit an organization's website nine times as often and view four times the number of pages as nonmembers (McKinsey).
- An estimated 66 percent of business decision-makers start purchase research at a search engine. Even more, 69 percent use Social Media (Motorola).

## Social Media Is Replacing Traditional Media Sources

It is clear from these statistics that Social Media has become a way of life that will only grow in importance in the future. In 2011, Social Media became the number-one channel for marketing spending by major organizations, according to the HubSpot "2012 State of Inbound Marketing" report. It also found that the top marketing channels from a generation ago, such as print, display, outdoor, and television, have moved near the bottom of the list for channel investment. Simply said, with the increased investment in and interest of the world in Social Media, its communities are fast becoming the number-one way for business-to-business (B2B), business-to-consumer (B2C), and business-to-business-to-consumer (B2B2C) organizations to exchange information internally and externally with their customers and prospects.

How hot is Social Media? Consider these findings:

1. When ISM conducted research for a major pharmaceutical customer, they learned that "Over 80% of Internet consumers search online for health information, trusting peer-generated Social Media content more than pharma company websites and what their physicians say."

   This was a shocking discovery. It's not a stretch to say that soon, if pharma and physician are removed from this quote, it could apply to just about any industry. This means that more than 80 percent of consumers will search online for information pertaining to an organization, and they will trust peer-generated content in Social Media communities more than information on an organization's website or so-called experts in that field. In several industries, including travel and healthcare, this behavior is already taking hold.

2. Every minute of every day:[1]
   - Facebook users share 2.5 million pieces of content,
   - Email users send 204 million messages,
   - Apple users download 48 thousand apps,
   - Google receives 4 million search queries,
   - YouTube users upload 72 hours of new video,
   - Twitter users tweet 277 thousand times,
   - and Amazon makes $83,000 in online sales.

3. The influence of Social Media continues to increase:[2]
   - 46% of web users look toward Social Media when making a purchase
   - 8 out of 10 SMB (small and medium businesses) use Social Media to drive growth

- 3 in 5 SMB say they've gained new customers by using Social Media
- 67% of Twitter users are far more likely to buy from the brands they follow on Twitter

## Meaningful Challenges Still Apply to Social Media and Social CRM

Social Media's impressive rise comes with meaningful challenges in the Social Media world. One challenge is that whereas good information travels quickly, bad information can travel even more quickly. Consider these faux pas when Social Media began to take hold in the marketplace:

- **New York City Police Department**—In April 2014, the NYPD asked Twitter users to share photos of themselves and NYPD officers, using the hashtag #myNYPD. But just a few days after this initiative, the NYPD was forced to rethink its Social Media strategy after users deluged this hashtag with inane and profane photos of NY police officers.
- **DHL Express**—In October 2014, DHL asked for "likes" within its Facebook account regarding recovery wishes for racecar driver Jules Bianchi's injuries caused by a crash in the Grand Prix. Facebook users immediately criticized DHL for the move, labeling it "tasteless" and "inappropriate," prompting the company to delete the post and issue an apology via Facebook.
- **American Apparel**—In late 2012, American Apparel offered a 20 percent discount on all items as a means of alleviating boredom among shoppers during the hurricane season. Perspective customers worldwide were appalled, after the destructiveness of Hurricane Sandy, and took to Twitter, Facebook, and other Social Media websites to condemn the ill-considered marketing message, thereby causing management a huge PR nightmare.

Successful Social Media initiatives are grounded in a strategic business context whereby the organization looks to Social Media as toolsets that support one of three core business strategies (these strategies were initially proposed by Michael Treacy in his co-authored book *The Discipline of Market Leaders*):

- **Product Leadership**—Companies such as Procter & Gamble (P&G) use Social Media ideation tools to facilitate the creation and formulation of new ideas within Social Media forums that subject matter experts (SMEs) participate in. P&G has taken the lead in utilizing ideation platforms, with more than one-third of its product innovation ideas being generated in these platforms.

- **Operational Excellence**—Social Media may also be used to cultivate operational excellence by having end users provide customer/technical support within organizationally set guidelines and proper training, thereby helping to drive down costs and increase efficiencies. Hewlett-Packard uses this technique effectively—it has saved in excess of $10 million by integrating Social Media into its call center/customer service offerings.

- **Customer Intimacy**—Social Media can also be used to boost customer intimacy by creating a two-way dialogue with constituents (such as customers or distribution partners) with the objective of deepening customer relationships and increasing an organization's growth engine. Dozens of best-in-class B2B and B2C organizations (for example, ExxonMobil and Amazon) are currently using Social Media to achieve customer intimacy.

Of these three business strategies, the biggest impact of Social Media is on customer intimacy. I recommend applying the Hub and Spoke Integrated Social Media model to make this impact (see Figure 1.1).

Organizations use publically available Social Media tools such as Facebook and Twitter with this model to drive traffic to their corporate website, which in turn is the best tool for driving traffic to their private Social Media community. A private Social Media community is where the company sponsors SME blogs, as well as community forums, best practices, polls, and contests of interest to their customers and prospects. This integrated Social Media approach helps to build the two-way dialogue between organizations and customers. It also allows organizations to harvest comments and other relevant information noted on their private social community and places these insights into customer and prospect profiles located within the organizations' Social CRM system. This allows them not only to have transactional information about their customers (for example, what they have purchased in the past and when), but also sentiment information (for example, what they like or dislike about doing business with the organization, opportunities they would like the organization to pursue, and so on).

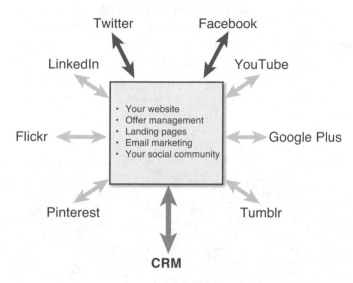

**Figure 1.1** The Hub and Spoke Integrated Social Media model

For example, an organization might choose to invite customers and prospects to a private social community discussion forum to learn more about what products or services its customers may be interested in. It can then harvest appropriate information from the forum and enter this information into individual customer profiles contained within the Social CRM system for use when marketing, selling, or servicing these customers or prospects. The organization can also use the data analytics tools (either within its Social CRM system or external data analytics tools) to understand trends gathered during forums, polls, contests, and so on, and feed these results back to the private social community in the form of information, products, or services, thus further enhancing the two-way dialogue.

## Sample Customer Profile

The customer profile is the core of every successful Social CRM implementation because it provides a holistic picture of a customer. Think of the profile as a daisy, where you put the customer in the center of the daisy and you have petals of information attached to the center. The sample customer profile shown in Figure 1.2 provides sample information petals for a pharmaceutical company's customer profile, with both traditional information petals (including customer information, activities, products purchased, financials, operational issues, service issues, customer insight, competitive information, marketing campaigns/ opportunities, and customer news) and the new Social Media information petal. To ensure appropriate security, all information petals can be can be turned on or off, depending on who is viewing the profile (that is, internal personnel or the customer).

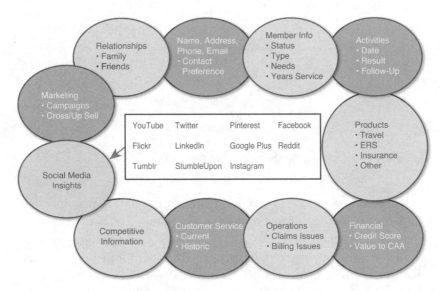

**Figure 1.2** SCRM Customer Profile

A customer profile that contains only traditional information holds essentially static information (that is, information that has taken place). By adding Social Media insights to a traditional customer profile gathered from Social Media blogs, community forums, ratings, polls, and so on, the organization now has static as well as positive and negative sentiment information that will provide a more holistic understanding of the customer relationship en route to achieving customer intimacy. The many organizations that have added the Social Media insight petal to their Social CRM customer profile have noted a higher level of sensitivity in the customer buy-cycle and a more effective approach to the organization's sell-cycle with the customer—both components of a more meaningful two-way dialogue with the customer.

## The American Automobile Association: A Successful Social Media/Social CRM Case Study

In the early 1990s, CRM was advertised as a panacea for organizations' sales and marketing woes. From ISM's research it is clear there has been a similar over-evangelizing of the Social Media effects on organizations. Yet, there are concrete, successful examples of implementations that ISM has participated in that highlight how Social Media can be used to assist an organization to grow its business and achieve a higher level of customer intimacy that leads to higher customer satisfaction, loyalty, and advocacy.

One example of this is in ISM's work with the American Automobile Association (AAA) to help design and implement six different Social Media communities during 2009 and 2010, several of which still exist today. These communities had the goal of deepening AAA's customer relationships and ultimately driving additional revenue to the AAA clubs. Several of these social communities were set up to feed information directly into AAA customer—or member—profiles contained within the Social CRM systems. The following are some pragmatic outcomes from two of these communities.

For one AAA club, ISM helped design and implement a Social Media "savings" community, aimed at helping this club's members who were suffering from the Great Recession. The concept was to engage in a conversation with members about how they can save using AAA's Show Your Card & Save (SYCS) program and other special deals made available within the community. The target audience for this community was members and prospects of all ages in a multistate geography, particularly people with a strong focus on savings. The community's goals were to expand the relationship with members, increase the perceived value of an AAA membership, and support increased sales. The Social Media tools initially used included a blog by SMEs, along with a contest to determine who saved the most from AAA's SYCS card program or had the best savings story. This AAA club also used forums to gather information on both member experiences using their AAA SYCS card and new potential vendors that wished to join the community. ISM carefully measured the impact of this community on customer satisfaction and enhanced revenues. The impact on both fronts proved very meaningful.

For the second AAA club, ISM helped analyze information coming from blogs and forums on its Social Media community and brought these insights directly into its Social CRM application and to the appropriate member profiles. This led to deeper insight into each member based on preferences gathered though the Social Media community and ultimately to enhanced and new product and service offerings.

ISM made a point to set up success metrics from the outset to determine the impact of these Social Media efforts on customer relationships to ensure that these communities delivered measurable value, not hype. This led to a lot of discussion within the six AAA clubs because at that time (and still today) many Social Media industry evangelists felt that making money from Social Media communities was not the right success metric. I vehemently disagreed, and asked, "Didn't we learn anything from the dot-com bust in the early 2000s?" So, for the AAA Social Media communities, ISM set out to measure new revenues generated from AAA members participating in the Social Media community compared to those who were not participating in the Social Media community. By measuring the sales lift between these two groups, AAA was in a position to cost-justify the expense of designing, implementing, and monitoring its Social Media communities. This type of business approach to Social Media will help ensure the overall success of this newly emerging industry.

Other AAA clubs benefited by directly integrating social insights from their private social communities into their Social CRM system. Some clubs now harvest relevant comments from social community users and add those comments to appropriate customer profiles. The comments can then be retrieved from a customer profile and used to provide deeper insights into the customer's emotional perspective for certain AAA products and services and/or automobile and travel issues. Ultimately, AAA's social-community effort has led to a better understanding and a closer relationship between AAA clubs and their members.

## Ensuring the Impact of Social Media on Customer Relationships

Clearly there is real value in creating a Social Media community and harvesting information generated on the community for use within an organization's Social CRM efforts. ISM helped to design Kraft Foodservice division's Social Media community with the goal of creating a two-way dialogue with chefs and restaurants owners. Similar to P&G's use of ideation tools offered within Social Media communities to generate product enhancements, Kraft's community will be a great place to test product ideas and to gather meaningful feedback that in turn will feed into its Social CRM system to help achieve customer intimacy.

Sticking with the linkage between Social Media communities and their impact on Social CRM, some organizations leverage their Social Media communities to create customer advocates, who in turn help promote products to other potential customers both within and outside the community. Other organizations use Social Media communities to save money on the support side by allowing properly trained customers to help fellow customers, rather than spending valuable internal resources on those support efforts.

An organization embarking on a Social Media initiative must have a well-planned strategy that supports the organization's core business goals. As information is gathered from a variety of feeds, including both public and private Social Media communities, it is important to have carefully thought through how the organization will integrate this information inside its current Social CRM system and how the organization will use this information to deepen customer relationships en route to achieving meaningful customer intimacy.

To successfully leverage Social Media to help achieve customer intimacy, here is a short list of actions an organization must include en route to achieving meaningful impact:

- Support the organization's business goals with Social Media.
- Define success for the community from the outset using clear metrics.
- Link Social Media efforts to existing Social CRM customer programs and outreach.
- Integrate Social Media with other marketing programs.
- Leverage existing internal organizational resources and initiatives.
- Monitor social communities carefully.
- Respond quickly to social community input.

The chapters that follow offer a comprehensive understanding of the current CRM, Social CRM, and Social Media marketplace and cover topics ranging from smart ways to incorporate Social Media into the enterprise to leveraging Social Media information to advance any organization's CRM efforts. They provide insight into how other organizations have achieved specific goals via best practices in Social CRM, and they help in overcoming skepticism so that any organization can exploit the real benefits of Social CRM.

## Endnotes

1. Domo, "Data Never Sleeps 2.0," http://www.domo.com/blog/2014/04/data-never-sleeps-2-0/ (April 23, 2014).

2. MarketingTechBlog, "2014 Statistics and Trends for Businesses on Social Media," https://www.marketingtechblog.com/2014-statistics-trends-businesses-social-media/ (October 1, 2014).

# 2

## Smart Ways to Incorporate Social Media into Your Organization

Social Media can be described as a strategy or tool for connecting with others. It can be used as a way to drive organizational information to customers, acquire information about existing customers, and obtain new customers. The value of Social Media is interacting with people to obtain information for potential marketing purposes, given that Social Media is an excellent way to communicate with customers and prospects as well as to gain insight into their behavior. "Networking" has gone on almost as long as societies have existed, but the unparalleled potential of the Internet to promote social connections via Social Media is only now being fully recognized and exploited.

## Empowering an Organization with Social Media

The millennial generation has embraced Social Media as an efficient way to communicate both professionally and personally. It is time for organizations to follow millennials and embrace it, too. Just like an enterprise resource planning (ERP) or CRM system, Social Media should be taken seriously and integrated into an organization's go-to-market strategy. But at present, many organizations do not know how best to adopt Social Media and incorporate it into their business strategies. Simply creating a Facebook, LinkedIn, or Twitter profile is not sufficient to establish a Social Media presence in today's marketplace. The following are four smart ways to incorporate Social Media into an organization.

### Social Listening and Engagement Tools

Apply digital-listening software to a public or private social community to track and analyze social sentiment regarding what customers and prospects are saying about you, your products, your services, and so on. Here's a good example of social listening and engagement tools in action:

> A few years ago, two newlyweds checked into a Ritz Carlton hotel in Las Vegas for their honeymoon. They were excited to be in Sin City and at the lovely Ritz Carlton property. Ritz Carlton placed them into a lovely room with wood paneling, a fireplace, and beautiful furniture (the typical Ritz Carlton setting). The bride went on her Twitter account and tweeted to her friends that "We finally arrived to our hotel, but it is not what I was expecting. I had hoped for a room with a big window that overlooked the Las Vegas strip. After all, this is my honeymoon!" Fortunately, Ritz Carlton has a sophisticated social listening and engagement capability and within minutes was able to pick up this bride's tweet and send it to the hotel manager in Las Vegas. A few minutes later a Ritz Carlton manager knocked on the newlywed's door and said, "You know, we have been thinking about you. You are a newly married couple and have come all the way to Las Vegas for your honeymoon. We think you would be better in one of our corner rooms, with modern furniture and with windows on all sides of the room overlooking the Las Vegas strip. Would that be okay for you?" A short while afterward, now settled in the new "modern" room overlooking the Las Vegas strip, the bride tweeted her friends saying, "You are not going to believe what just happened. The manager of the hotel knocked on our door and offered us a gorgeous corner room with large glass windows on all sides overlooking the strip. The view is outrageous! What a great hotel!"

Social listening and engagement tools are most often used on public social communities (for example, Facebook, Twitter, and so on) to capture the voice of the customer, to help identify and target key influencers, and to expand channel coverage and scope.

### Private Social Media Communities

Organizations increasingly are building private Social Media communities. Private Social Media communities are very similar to public Social Media communities with one major exception: Private social communities are not open to everyone, but rather are targeted to customer groups with which organizations are keen to create a two-way communication. Many software platforms are available to build private Social

Media communities (for example, Jive, Lithium, Mzinga, and Zimbra). Private Social Media communities are typically accessible via invitation from the organization's website, although organizations are using the hub-and-spoke model described in Chapter 1, "Social CRM: The Intersection of Social Media and CRM," to leverage public Social Media communities to promote their private communities and entice new customers and prospects to join them.

The value of a private Social Media community versus a public community is that the organization owns the data being generated on the community, which is important for effective Social CRM. The organization also has a large say about who joins the community, as well as a meaningful say on the rules and regulations of the community. Last, private Social Media communities are owned by the organization and are considerably less likely to be blocked by some countries that still ban public Social Media communities.

The value-add of the private Social Media community is that the organization can target topical communications to its customers and prospects via blogs, forums, polls, contests, and so on. The community can also distribute customer-facing collateral on the community (for example, proof of performance data sheets). Private Social Media communities are also rich environments for creating platforms for innovation using ideation tools (for example, run a contest that asks customers to share their most creative use of a product, and the winner gets something for being the most innovative).

### Enterprise Collaboration (Knowledge Communities)

The first two smart ways to incorporate Social Media into an organization are external facing; the next two are internal facing. Enterprise collaboration, or knowledge communities, leverage Social Media tools to facilitate easy sharing of information among personnel. In knowledge communities, personnel worldwide can search for and connect to internal SMEs to address issues, generate referrals and introductions leading to new potential business, and collaborate and solve customer challenges by sharing what has worked elsewhere. The organization can capture the voice of the employee so that valuable knowledge (for example, customer, market, and competitive) stays within the organization. According to an AARP survey (discussed in its 2011 "Employee Experiences and Expectations: Finding, Training and Keeping Qualified Employees" report) of more than 1,000 HR directors, 24 percent of employees said that they are very concerned about losing knowledge and critical experience as their organizations' older workers retire. And according to the Career Partners International 2010 "Mature Workforce" survey, at least 90 percent of respondents in every sector expect retirements to significantly increase the loss of knowledge and experience. Enterprise collaboration has come into vogue thanks to tools such as Salesforce.com's Chatter and Microsoft's Yammer, which are platforms designed to provide similar Facebook- and Twitter-style collaboration capabilities for users within an organization. Users of Chatter or Yammer can create and access profiles, set up meetings or groups with other members of an organization, and provide status updates and share content, files, and real-time feeds with other users in the organization. For example, a Chatter or Yammer newsfeed can display alerts of changes to records and new announcements with other members of an organization.

An example of an effective use of enterprise collaboration is to use Chatter or Yammer to set up an internal community-selling environment, where shared intellectual selling is encouraged. Internal staff then can cooperate to help close sales opportunities or resolve customer issues.

### Channel and Partner Collaboration

Channel and partner collaboration is the fourth smart way to incorporate Social Media into an organization. Leveraging Social Media tools, the goal of channel and partner collaboration is to open a two-way dialogue with your channel members and partners. This includes, for example, sharing and qualifying priority sales leads, developing customer-facing collateral, executing go-to-market strategies, and capturing the voice of the partner.

Microsoft is an effective user of partner collaboration tools. Microsoft built ExpertZone for the sales reps of its retail partners (for example, Best Buy, GameStop, and Target) to help coordinate partner training and collaboration. ExpertZone uses several Social Media tools to entice retail partners to participate in the ExpertZone community. They include badging, friendly competitions among members, leaderboards and competitions within the leaderboards, gamification, and more.

I work closely with many global customers—including ExxonMobil, Ferguson, Johnson Controls, and Kraft Foods—to help them review and/ or set up channel-and-partner collaboration capabilities. For example, ExxonMobil opened its Mobil SHC Club private social community to its

Equipment Builder partners, and Kraft Foods is working on ways to use Social Media to engage its key distributors.

## Use a Phased Approach to Introduce Social Media into the Organization

For Social Media to be useful, it must be used in a group context in which all parties have a mutual interest to benefit from one another. A successful Social Media initiative is strategic about how to use the collaboration and innovation available from Social Media to benefit the organization. This includes both internal staff and external customer benefits coming from Social Media communities.

Management should realize that some people will resist using Social Media. A Social Media initiative can also be problematic if it creates too much change for the organization's staff. With this in mind, in the first phase management should first look for small wins by identifying Social Media activists within departments or within customer groups who will help drive initial success of the Social Media community. Management should also identify employees who leverage popular Social Media applications to assist them with their day-to-day work. For example, HR departments should use LinkedIn as a valuable tool to assist with hiring new employees and conducting background checks. The sales department can also leverage LinkedIn and Facebook for lead generation and qualification. PR and marketing personnel are increasingly turning to Twitter for generating outbound communications.

Once there are sufficient Social Media users, the organization is ready to create either an external community (public or private) or an internal community (enterprise collaboration or channel-and-partner collaboration) to help secure the benefits noted previously. In successive Social Media phases, the organization leverages learning from previous phases to deepen its two-way communication with customers and/or to enhance internal collaboration.

## Making Money from Social Media

Social Media return on investment (ROI) continues to baffle many organizations. An eConsultancy survey of 1,000 organizations and agencies in 2012 discussed in its "State of Social" report that 41 percent of respondents had no idea how to measure Social Media's financial impact.

At the same time, a 2011 digital marketing forecast by Gartner estimated that by the end of 2015, organizations would generate 50 percent of web sales via their social presence and mobile applications. Companies such as Amazon, Zappos, and many others have already met and exceeded these forecasts.

So it is fair to ask, can you really make money from a successful Social Media effort, and if the answer is yes, how do you measure the ROI? My response is yes, and here are two ways to accomplish revenue generation using Social Media.

## Hub-and-Spoke Model

Communities such as Facebook, LinkedIn, and Twitter already have millions of members, so organizations will inevitably be attracted to creating their Social Media communities on these public platforms. I previously described the hub-and-spoke model in Chapter 1. This model calls for the organization to use these public communities to promote the brand and to share news with followers, but most important, to drive traffic from the public community to the private Social Media community, enabling the organization to filter relevant social insights directly into the Social CRM system for targeted customer engagement.

For example, during its work with Kraft's Foodservice division, ISM learned that restaurant chefs were hesitant to share valuable information regarding Kraft products on open communities such as Facebook, but that they were willing to share valuable information on a private Kraft community, where they can confidentially trade recipes, swap stories, and share other cooking information with their peers. Furthermore, Kraft is more likely to be in a position to influence the purchase decisions of chefs within their own community, rather than on a Facebook community visited by their competitors (and who may not even be a part of Kraft's targeted audience).

One example of an ISM customer using the hub-and-spoke model to make money using Social Media is the American Automobile Association (AAA) and one of its Social Media member communities.

When several AAA clubs readied to launch their Social Media communities, one club requested that I work with it to learn more about how different cohorts wanted information presented on the emerging Social Media community. I learned that mature adults wanted AAA to present their information by lifestyle, whereas teenagers and young adults wanted information presented by topic.

The management of this AAA club leveraged this valuable insight to modify its social community implementation so that it would be more lively and exciting for those who visited the community. By analyzing data from the social community—including which members visited which parts of the community, what comments were made by which members in which forums, and so on—AAA was able to enhance its products, services, and marketing efforts to help secure more business from existing and new members. Meanwhile, the club gathered social insight from members participating in the community and placed this insight into its Social CRM system for appropriate member engagement. Of greatest importance, this AAA club measured the lift in sales from participating community members versus nonparticipating members to determine community ROI.

Key reasons for this AAA Social Media member community's success include the following:

- The Social Media community directly supported AAA's business goals, which included deepening AAA member relationships.
- From the start, the AAA staff carefully monitored the social community and responded quickly to member input.
- AAA management defined success using clear metrics. Although community metrics such as revenue growth, the number of threads, and how many people are responding to threads are important, most important was the club's decision to compare revenue from community members to revenue from non-community members to determine the ROI for the community.
- AAA proactively linked the community to existing Social CRM member programs and integrated the community with other AAA marketing programs.
- Feedback from the AAA social community has led to changes in specific AAA marketing programs, which in turn have helped ensure meaningful ROI.

## Social Media–Enabled Applications

Social Media–enabled business applications will also contribute to organizations making money via Social Media. Many more organizations in the future will offer Social Media–enabled business applications in the areas of sales, customer service, and marketing. Royal Bank of Canada (RBC) and 1-800-Flowers are two examples of this growing trend.

RBC added analytics to its customer service model. The bank has moved from a relatively low customer satisfaction score of 5 to a high score of 1 by providing customer service reps with information about life-changing events for their clients gathered in part from their social profiles. Knowing life-changing events, such as when the client moves, marries, has a baby, and so on, has helped RBC refine its marketing efforts and generate sales. In the other example, 1-800-Flowers came up with different gift ideas for occasions such as Mother's Day and Father's Day to help grow its business by using Social Media–influenced concepts such as crowdsourcing, ideation, and collective intelligence.

Organizations have also begun to embed Social Media–enabled applications into their internal operations. HR organizations are using Social Media–enabled applications to attract and retain talent and to motivate and inspire personnel.

Here are the key takeaways for organizations wanting to incorporate Social Media and make money from it:

- There are four smart ways to incorporate Social Media into an organization: social listening and engagement tools, private Social Media communities, enterprise collaboration (knowledge communities), and channel and partner collaboration.

- Use a phased approach to introduce Social Media into the organization.

- Use the hub-and-spoke model to drive customers and prospects from public Social Media communities to the organization's private social community. Then gather filtered social insights coming from the private community and place them into the organization's Social CRM system to achieve enhanced customer engagement.

- Consider adding Social Media–enabled applications to external functions, such as sales, marketing, and customer service, as well as to internal functions, including HR.

- Ensure that the Social Media initiative is tightly linked to delivering the organization's business goals. Then set up meaningful financial metrics at the outset of the initiative and monitor these metrics monthly.

Chapter 3, "Social Media Pilot Case Study," looks deeply into at a Social Media pilot case study that successfully incorporated many of the previously mentioned points.

# 3

## Social Media Pilot Case Study

ISM implemented a global Social Media pilot at one of its customer companies, referred to here as Front Runner. This customer is a well-known brand that provides products and services to consumers worldwide. During this journey, ISM planned, designed, and implemented the pilot, learning lessons along the way.

Front Runner saw Social Media as a new way to communicate with and relate to employees, consumers, partners, and other stakeholders. Using Social Media tools, Front Runner created an online community that allows its customers and prospects to get information, opinions, solutions, and ratings directly from each other rather than from other organizations.

## Social Media Plan

The journey started with the creation of Front Runner's Social Media plan, which contained the following five steps:

### Step 1: Constituency Selection

Front Runner first selected the constituency it wanted to work with during the six-month pilot. The company considered internal employees, customers, partners that it works with, prospects, and even prospective employees. After much consideration, Front Runner subsidiaries selected customers and prospects as the constituency of choice.

### Step 2: Technographic Profiling

Front Runner next undertook the task of determining this constituency's *technographic* profile. Technographic profiling is a way to segment a customer base and is particularly relevant when designing and implementing a Social Media initiative. It is similar to demographic or psychographic segmentation, but focuses on the technology-related behavior of an individual. Several technographic scales, spectrums, and ladders are now available to segment individuals based on their use of technology, including whether they are active Social Media participants. Forrester Research created one such ladder a few years ago. At one end of the ladder are the creators of blogs, videos, and so on; in the middle there are the joiners who tag web pages, use RSS feeds, and so on; and at the other end of the ladder are the inactives who sit on the sideline and opt not to actively participate in the Social Media boom. Front Runner wanted to perform technographic profiles to determine which customers and prospects would be most likely to participate in the Social Media pilot and how best to approach and engage these constituents in the pilot.

Front Runner gathered the names, physical addresses, and email addresses of potential customers and prospects it felt might be good pilot candidates to come up with the technographic profiles. Next, it did a third-party data overlay, and sent the name, physical address, and email address of the customers and prospects to a third-party data vendor (for example, Axiom or Experian). The vendor continuously compiles lots of information about individuals taken from a variety of sources—financials, purchases, social activities, demographics, lifestyle information, Social Media participation, and so on. The third-party vendor needed the name, physical address, and/or email address of Front Runner's customers and prospects, which are then used to perform the overlay to determine where each customer and prospect falls in the technographic ladder (that is, creators, joiners, and inactives). The exercise allowed Front Runner to identify constituents who it thought would be the most active participants during the Social Media pilot. In turn, Front Runner sent special invitations and incentives to the creators and joiners to encourage them to take a leading role in the pilot program.

I do not recommend embarking on a Social Media initiative until completing some level of technographic profiling. In Front Runner's case, because it was creating a global pilot, part of the challenge was getting meaningful third-party overlays for all 5,000 potential customers and prospects considered for the pilot. Different regions of the world and even different countries within these regions have differing data privacy policies that impact the ability to arrive at meaningful technographic profiles. ISM came up with a list everyone was comfortable with in view of these restrictions.

### Step 3: Business Goal Identification and Community Metrics

Next, ISM and Front Runner had to lock down the business goals for the pilot. There are many potential goals for a Social Media initiative—some technical and some business focused. For example, in their best-selling book *Groundswell,* Forrester's Charlene Li and Josh Bernoff write about Social Media business strategies that include customer listening (researching), talking (marketing), energizing (sales), supporting (support), and embracing (product development).

It took a while for the global Front Runner team to agree on metrics for the pilot, but the goal-selection process was critical to the long-term success of the pilot. As Peter Drucker reminds us, "If you can't measure it, you can't manage it." Here are the goals that Front Runner executives agreed to for the pilot:

- Five hundred registered users by the end of the pilot period.
- One hundred posts per month by the final month of the pilot.
- Quarter-over-quarter increase in time spent on the site and number of page views.
- Annual industrial brand satisfaction survey results with a higher satisfaction score for community members versus nonmembers.
- End-pilot community survey showing positive impact of the community on member satisfaction and value of the community.
- Increase in sales by 0.5 percent by the end of the pilot, resulting from customer participation in the Social Media community. Sales lift to be determined by measuring sales growth of community members versus that of nonmembers.

### Step 4: Vendor Selection

While ISM was guiding Front Runner in the design and implementation of the Social Media pilot, ISM also facilitated the process of selecting a Social Media vendor platform for use by Front Runner in the implementation of the pilot. There are many solid Social Media platform vendors in the market—Jive, Lithium, Mzinga, and Zimbra, and so on. The challenge was to come up with appropriate business and technical criteria in preparation for the vendor shootout we facilitated.

I have performed vendor-software selection for ISM clients for many years, and we had an awesome Front Runner vendor-selection team in place, so we were confident that we had identified all requirements. It turned out that the winning vendor had not been entirely honest during the shootout about its business analytics capabilities (which is important for measuring community metrics), but other than this factor, the vendor-selection process went flawlessly.

## Step 5: Community Engagement Plan

Developing the community engagement plan was the next step in the realizing the Front Runner pilot. A Social Media community engagement plan typically describes the following:

- An overview of the pilot.
- The pilot's business goals, objectives, and metrics.
- The target audience.
- The Social Media technology tools to be used.
- User access to the community (for example, a unique URL, from the Front Runner website, from public Social Media communities, and so on).
- The communication vehicles that will be used to promote the community (for example, local media, the sales force, regional marketing teams, and so on) as well as the sequencing of agreed-on promotional messages building up to the pilot. (In Front Runner's case, there was another layer of complexity: All communications had to be done in multiple languages.)
- How business partners will contribute during the pilot (for example, act as community members, SMEs, facilitators of forums, and so on).
- A description of who will fill the various pilot roles, including project owner, project manager, community manager, partner manager, technical lead, moderator, and administrator.
- A timeline containing all action items needed for a successful pilot program.

# Pilot Description

**Primary objective**: Increase customer loyalty and advocacy by engaging in a digital conversation with customers and prospects that drives Front Runner sales and increases Front Runner's brand strength.

**Secondary objective**: Harvest comments made on the social community, load them into Front Runner's CRM application, and share these insights with Front Runner's sales, marketing, customer service, and product development personnel.

**Audience**: Global customers and prospects who are fans of Front Runner's products and services, who are credible, and who have a strong technographic profile.

**Duration**: 6 months

**Tools**: A private Social Media community tool that contains the following items:

- A searchable FAQ/knowledge base
- An "Ask Front Runner" Google-like search box responded to by Front Runner (SMEs) to get questions answered in a timely manner
- Industry trends report
- Quick survey/polling tool
- Multiple blogs authored by both internal and external SMEs
- Forums about technical topics of interest to Front Runner's customer base
- A video contest to select the most innovative user of Font Runner products and services

# Lessons Learned

Readying for and implementing the Front Runner pilot was an interesting journey. All pilot metrics—both community and business—were met. Post-pilot customer surveys also confirmed increased customer engagement, advocacy, and satisfaction. As a result, the pilot was deemed a big success, permitting the Front Runner executive team to formally launch the community shortly after the pilot's completion. The community has since become a key component of Front Runner's global market reach. Here are the top lessons learned along the way:

- *Secure community sponsorship at the highest levels.* To secure support from Front Runner executives, the Social Media community had to tightly support the organization's global business goals and objectives. This was a challenging process, but one well worth the effort.

- *Create community metrics at the outset and measure them on a regular basis.* Unlike most consumer Social Media sites that are still searching for a business model that generates revenue, from the outset Front Runner's global Social Media community focused on establishing both standard community metrics (participation, growth in content, and so on) and, more important, business benefit metrics that included deepened penetration within key segments of the customer base and new customer revenues.

- *Integrate the Social Media community with other ongoing initiatives.* Front Runner's Social Media community was not launched as a standalone island. Instead, the community was designed to seamlessly integrate with existing Front Runner customer and prospect marketing outreach programs that utilized existing internal resources. Many Front Runner employees were also invited to participate in the community. This helped secure needed backing for the community from Front Runner's global executive team.

- *Leverage external channel partners.* Front Runner decided to invite partners and distribution channel members to participate in the community. These third parties were invited to write blogs, participate in forums, and sponsor contests within the community. Front Runner was able to add subject matter expertise and additional horsepower to community efforts by leveraging external resources.

- *Community monitoring needs to be taken very seriously.* Front Runner spent a lot of time pondering how best to monitor and moderate the Social Media community. Although Social Media platform tools allow organizations to filter comments for appropriateness, the community needs to be monitored on a regular basis for accuracy and civility. ISM shared monitoring responsibilities with Front Runner during the pilot, and together everyone learned how to counter self-promotion or inflammatory statements without taking away from the spontaneity of the community.

- *Global communities have additional complexities.* Being a global community added many challenges, including working across multiple time zones, being sensitive to differing data privacy laws in different countries, and listening carefully to a wide range of business requirements.

- *Social Media community integration with Social CRM is still not intuitive.* The harvesting and integration of social insights gathered from Front Runner's social community proved a big challenge. As a result, Front Runner is currently putting into place a more automated process to harvest social insights gathered from the community, integrate them into its Social CRM application, and then to leverage these insights in its customer engagement efforts.

Part II of *The Definitive Guide to Social CRM* focuses on the optimal Social CRM framework for organizations, along with the methods of leveraging Social Media communities in support of Social CRM, the benefits of Social Media knowledge communities for Social CRM, and ways of overcoming skepticism to exploit Social CRM.

# Part II
## Social CRM

# 4

## Leverage Social Media Information to Advance Your Social CRM Efforts

Social Media is having a tremendous impact on business throughout the world. The transformational phenomenon of Social Media is forcing organizations to adapt and build a definitively more customer-centered focus. The increasing use of Social Media tools and techniques is also driving organizations to leverage Social Media information as a means of progressing in their CRM efforts. Prior to digging into each of the four major steps of the Social CRM framework that I use throughout *The Definitive Guide to Social CRM*, the framework requires an exacting definition (see Figure 4.1).

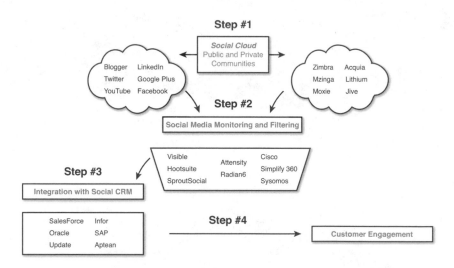

**Figure 4.1** The Social CRM framework

# Step 1: Monitor Social Media Communities to Glean Social Insights

More than 200 monitoring tools are available that listen to up to 150 million Social Media websites and communities daily. Think of Social Media monitoring tools as digital crawlers that listen to designated Social Media communities for keywords, tone, sentiment, volume, demographics, location, influencer status, and more. For example, Marriott might want to know who is saying nice things and who is saying not-so-nice things about the hotel chain or one of its 18 brands—which range from Fairfield Inn & Suites to the Ritz Carton—on Social Media communities. Marriott might also want to know which of these comments are coming from Marriott Platinum Elite customers or customers that have a Marriott Rewards credit card.

At present, most of the monitoring tools work only on public Social Media communities (for example, Facebook, Twitter, and others). These tools capture social insight and store it for further use, as we will discuss later. In Marriott's case, based on what it hears using listening tools, it may very well want to take immediate action to address issues that customers raise—remember the Ritz Carlton Tweet incident in Chapter 2, "Smart Ways to Incorporate Social Media into Your Organization"?

Several important questions should be asked regarding the use of Social Media monitoring tools:

**Question 1:** What should an organization monitor and which are the leading vendors that offer tools used to monitor Social Media communities?

For example, should Marriott focus on what people are saying about the overall Marriott brand, what people are saying about individual Marriott brands, or both? Should Marriott focus more on what is being said about Marriott brands or more on what is being said about competitive brands (for example, Choice, Hilton, InterContinental, Starwood, and others)? The short answer is, all of those things. An organization should monitor Social Media communities that have the greatest impact on its brand image and its go-to-market business strategy. How much emphasis an organization places on each depends on its goals for monitoring social conversations. Regarding leading vendors that offer Social Media monitoring tools, Appendix B, "Leading Social Media Monitoring and Filtering Tools," provides this list, along with some details on each vendor's offering.

**Question 2:** How much do Social Media monitoring tools cost and what ROI can one expect from using these tools?

Currently, many organizations are listening to Social Media communities, but few are listening well. According to survey data from Online Marketing Trends, here is how much people are spending for these tools:

- 55 percent—less than $100 per month
- 20 percent—between $100 and $500 per month
- 19 percent—between $500 and $5,000 per month
- 4 percent—between $5,000 and $10,000 per month
- 2 percent—$10,000 or more per month

These statistics suggest that currently, more than half of the respondents spend less than $100 per month monitoring social insights—insights that may positively or negatively impact the organization's brand or image. Although many organizations are still learning how to use these tools effectively, those that do use them well know that this Social Media monitoring cannot be a half-hearted effort. Two such organizations are Dell Computer Corp. and PepsiCo's Gatorade, which have optimized their use of Social Media listening tools and are showing a meaningful ROI on their monitoring tool investment.

In 2010 Dell's top management created a war room that the company calls its Social Media Command Center, in its Red Rock, Texas location. The command center has six large screens that monitor about 20,000 mentions in 12 languages regarding the Dell brand within key Social Media communities that include Twitter and Social Media blogs and forums. Dell has put in place strict procedures regarding how its employees are to respond when there are peaks in discussions about Dell products and services, so they can be quickly and properly be dealt with. These procedures prioritize responses for certain mentions of the Dell brand on Social Media communities and act on these mentions via Dell's Social CRM application. In Gatorade's case, it launched its Social Media mining tool center in January 2010. Dell and Gatorade are part of the pioneering 6 percent of organizations that are spending more than $5,000 per month to monitor Social Media in a serious manner.

Regarding ROI of monitoring tools, Dell has booked over $6.5 million on revenue-driving deals through @Delloutlet to its 1.57 million followers by making special offers to followers on Twitter.[1] Not a bad ROI! Here, some insight from one Dell executive regarding the company's Social Media listening efforts:

"It starts with listening. You need to understand your customers. Many marketing-driven campaigns are based on big ideas. Forget that. You need to listen and identify key influencers. Use your Social Media as a Social CRM platform. If you think about fans, likes, followers, and connections that you are developing, think about how you develop an engagement plan. And treat them the same way you would treat direct mail/email because it's exactly the same: You need to keep them interested and you need to keep getting the sales message out to them."

**Question 3:** Should an organization monitor public or private Social Media communities?

The short answer to this question is *both*, assuming they are available. The Social CRM framework diagram purposely shows both public and private Social Media communities. The pros of public Social Media communities include the fact that they are excellent forums for branding and for spreading information to a large quantity of existing and potential customers. The cons of public communities include the facts that organizations do not own the data generated in these communities; they do not control the community policies; there tends to be limited public intimacy (because in a public community, comments are accessible to everyone belonging to the community—and not everyone is comfortable with this scenario); and public communities are rarely a consumer destination to purchase products or services.

The pros of private Social Media communities are that organizations have the ability to open a two-way dialogue with and among their customers; they own the data within these communities; control community policies; restrict and control community membership; and heavily influence the design of the community to meet the organization's needs as well as the needs of its customers and prospects. The con of private communities is that it typically takes more time, money, and effort to plan and launch a private community.

The ideal situation is the hub-and-spoke model: An organization has a presence on public Social Media sites for branding and information dissemination purposes, while offering its customers the opportunity to join the company's private Social Media community, where they can have more intimate and meaningful exchanges with their peers.

Similarly, the ideal situation is for an organization to listen to what its customers are saying, harvest or scrape relevant social insight from both public and private Social Media communities, and then place this social insight into the appropriate place within its Social CRM system so that this insight can be used during the customer engagement process. Again, the answer is *both,* assuming that both public and private are available.

**Question 4:** What is the impact of data privacy when monitoring work is being performed?

Individuals and businesses increasingly are using data privacy settings contained within their public and private Social Media communities to block monitoring tools from capturing what they are saying in these communities. If privacy settings are blocking what someone is saying, there will be no social insight coming from that individual's community participation and therefore no input for Social CRM purposes. This is an increasingly important issue following several infamous data security breaches in both public and private sector organizations over the past few years. Moreover, the attention given to data privacy issues differs by geographical region worldwide, so some homework needs to be done to come up with a successful monitoring strategy. On the flip side, provided the organization has a responsible data privacy policy in place that is open to customer review, research confirms that once an organization has established trust with its customers regarding the accountable use of their data, those customers tend to be willing to share social insights with the organization.

## Step 2: Filter Social Media Insight

This Social CRM framework step is to filter what is being said in both public and private Social Media communities. How does filtering work? Let's assume for a moment we are a Samsung television brand manager. We might indicate on the Social Media filtering tool that we are interested in any mention—positive or negative—of a particular Samsung television brand. We can specify that we are not interested in competitive television brand names, or that we are interested in Samsung mentions on Twitter, but not on Facebook. For example, we can ask the tool to filter on any tweets or comments in public and private blogs that contain any mention of our particular Samsung television brand. The monitoring tool will then send out digital "crawlers" containing this filtered request to identified Twitter and private and public blogs and capture relevant comments that are being said about our specific Samsung television brand.

A state-of-the-art Social Media monitoring tool can leverage filtering to perform the following tasks:

- Monitor and capture filtered volume, demographics, location, tone, and sentiment of Social Media posts.

- Identify Social Media influencers (for example, SMEs).

- Monitor filtered comments from communities and blog accounts, all from one tool console.

- Provide for workflow management functionality (that is, automatically assign related Social Media incidents such as a customer service tweet to the appropriate staff for appropriate follow-up).

- Deliver spam management and text analysis of unstructured text.

- Auto-compare brand sentiment to competitors.

- Perform trend analysis and 3D graphical reporting.

It is not an easy job to use Social Media filtering tools to search for and document optimal keywords or keyword groups used within Social Media communities. Here's why: Most Social Media communities contain a lot of "free-form" text, which complicates keyword searching. Proximity searches within a Social Media community may also be complicated, as noted in the following free-form text example: "My commute to work in my Toyota Corolla stinks." Will the monitoring tool understand that the commute stinks or that the Toyota Corolla stinks? In this case, the interpretation by the monitoring tool can have a substantial impact on what is being understood and documented.

Monitoring tools also often fall short when comments on the Social Media community are ambiguous. For example, how will a monitoring tool interpret the comment, "Nike rocks"? Will the monitoring tool interpret the following comment positively or negatively: "I really like the Garmin GPS, but it is difficult to use." In filtering such ambiguous comments, the Social Media filtering application may not be able to determine the correct sentiment of such comments.

Additional filtering challenges include the following:

- Knowing how to set up the search criteria for each individual Social Media community (for example, Facebook, Twitter, and others).

- Twitter's 140 character limit challenges the monitoring tool to take into account some awkward abbreviations.

- Lingo is used in all communities; the monitoring tool must do its best to understand this lingo.

- Sentiment can be complicated: for example, a loyal Marriott member loves Ritz Carlton hotels but hates Fairfield Inns.

At present, Social Media filtering is a work in progress and will likely continue to be a challenge for many organizations in the foreseeable future.

## Step 3: Integrate Social Insight into an Organization's Social CRM Application

After the Social Media filtering process is complete, relevant Social Media insight is ready to be imported into the organization's Social CRM application for use in the organization's customer engagement process. The integration of social insight into an organization's Social CRM application is at the core of the Social CRM industry, which is the intersection of Social Media and Social CRM. Organizations now have a unique opportunity to leverage social insights in their sales, marketing, and customer service efforts. One example of Social CRM in action comes from Salesforce.com's Integrated Social CRM Toolset.

A leading global bank uses Salesforce.com's Radian6 monitoring tool to monitor customer tweets. The Radian6 tool identifies an unfavorable tweet from one of the bank's important customers. The Radian6 tool next creates a customer service case in Salesforce.com's Social CRM application that automatically gets routed to the right customer service rep within the bank for immediate action. The rep reaches out to the customer and resolves the issue. All notes associated with this incident are stored in the customer's profile that is housed within this bank's Salesforce.com application.

I have mentioned the importance of integrating social insight into the customer profiles housed within the Social CRM application. What follows the integration is a sample customer profile that is housed within the Social CRM application prior to and after social insight has been added to the profile (see Figures 4.2 and 4.3). After social insight has been added to the enhanced customer profile, the organization has a more complete understanding of the customer. In turn, the organization is in a better position to engage with the customer in ways that the customer will likely find to be more meaningful.

**Figure 4.2** Sample customer profile *before* social insight has been integrated

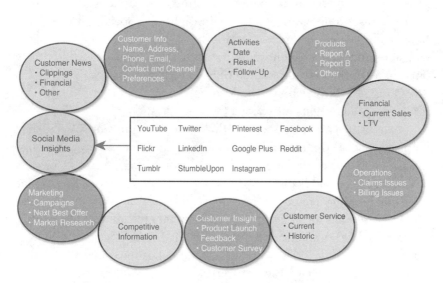

**Figure 4.3** Sample customer profile *after* social insight has been integrated

As with Step 1 (monitoring) and Step 2 (filtering), several important questions should be asked regarding the use of Step 3 (social insight integration):

**Question 1:** Should an organization integrate all social insight into the customer profile or some subset of it?

The current focus of many Social Media and Social CRM software vendors is to integrate customer service issues from public Social Media communities into the Social CRM application (similar to the example provided previously for Salesforce.com). Some vendors are focusing on sales insights and have made it quite easy, for example, to move sales lead information from a public Social Media community directly into the Social CRM application. There are fewer vendors that have focused on easily moving marketing insights gathered from public Social Media communities into the Social CRM application. This is a result in part from there being more free-form text as one moves from customer service through sales into marketing. As stated earlier, monitoring and filtering free-form text presents certain challenges. What's more, even fewer software vendors have done a good job preparing for the integration of social insights from private Social Media communities into Social CRM applications. This is a result, in part, from a lack of standards for the tools used in the Social Media platforms that vendors offer for building private Social Media communities. To summarize, although it will make a lot of sense to integrate most social insight into Social CRM applications in the future, the Social CRM industry is in the third inning of the ballgame, and there are still six innings to go. Much remains to be worked out regarding the easy integration of Social Media insights.

**Question 2:** Which are the leading vendors offering tools used to integrate social insights into Social CRM applications?

Two distinct types of Social CRM vendors are currently in the marketplace: Social Media vendors that offer comprehensive online community platforms containing social applications (blogs, forums, contests, polls, and so on) and Social CRM vendors that offer a Social Media platform for building online communities and afterward allowing for the import of relevant social insight information into the appropriate profiles in the Social CRM application. Appendix C, "Leading Social CRM Software Solutions," provides a list with some detail regarding the leading vendors offering Social CRM software.

**Question 3:** Is it easy to integrate social insight into a Social CRM application?

There are currently three ways to technically integrate social insight into a Social CRM application:

- Most vendors offer standard application programming interfaces (APIs) to achieve this integration.

- Some vendors have created business process flows and programmed this social insight integration directly into their software platform.

- Other vendors have written software to reach out to filtered social insight and pull this insight into their Social CRM application.

These integration approaches work, but improvements being made to them at this time will make them even easier to use in the future. Also, whereas today's integrations focus mainly on getting social insight into the Social CRM application, in the near future these integrations will easily deliver social insight directly into the appropriate customer petal(s) on the daisy profile contained within the Social CRM application.

**Question 4:** What is the optimal frequency to update social insights into the Social CRM application, and how far back in time should an organization go to gather social insight?

It should come as no surprise that there is no standard optimal frequency for updating social insight into a Social CRM application, given how young the Social CRM industry is. Some organizations update social insights daily or weekly; others do the updates monthly or quarterly. Best practices suggest that the updates should be done as often as meaningful changes in the social insight occur, which of course means that the organization needs to understand its customers and their Social Media behavior.

Typically, organizations go back 90 to 180 days to grab and maintain social insight data, but again, this depends in part on multiple factors—or example, special events that may have taken place between the organization and customers on Social Media communities.

## Step 4: Leveraging Social Insight to Achieve Enhanced Customer Engagement

In this last step of the Social CRM framework, the organization observes which Social Media channel the customer used to create the social insight, and then uses that channel to engage back with that customer. So, if the customer used the Facebook public Social Media community channel to post a comment, the organization engages that customer via that channel. The same applies in the case of the customer engaging the organization via a Twitter public Social Media community, via a private Social Media community, via public or private blogs, and so on.

The big challenge in leveraging social insight to achieve enhanced customer engagement revolves around the question, how do organizations best use social insight that is now stored in the Social CRM profile? This is by far the hardest question to answer because many "soft" issues affect the best use of social insight data. Organizations must be sensitive when using what they know about a customer. Customers do not want to feel as if they are being inappropriately tracked. Employees using Social CRM may also be reluctant to use social insight information in fear of making a mistake and looking foolish in front of the customer. My advice is that management create employee guidelines for those using Social CRM to help them understand and respect the sensitivity associated with customers' social insight information; that organizations train their Social CRM users on scenarios for when and when not to use social insight; and that management set aside the appropriate time to accomplish these important activities.

In Chapters 5–7, I examine several of the challenges and opportunities associated with the effective use of this Social CRM framework.

# Endnotes

1.  FT Press, "How to Make Money with Social Media: In the Beginning," http://www.ftpress.com/articles/article.aspx?p=2240520 (August 13, 2014).

# 5

# Creating Your Social Media Community in Support of Social CRM

In Chapter 2, "Smart Ways to Incorporate Social Media into Your Organization," I introduced private Social Media communities as one of the four smart ways to introduce Social Media into the organization. I also suggested that private Social Media communities are an essential component in the Social CRM Framework. In this chapter, we dig deeper into the value of Social Media communities, particularly private Social Media communities.

## Why Create a Social Media Community?

Here are the key reasons why organizations create Social Media communities:

- **To grow revenues**—Research shows that members of a Social Media community are more engaged with the organization sponsoring the community and consequently are more likely to buy products/services from that organization than nonmembers. It is not atypical for Social Media Community members to purchase 10 to 15 percent more products than non-community members.

- **To decrease costs**—The price of engagement using a Social Media community runs at a fraction of the cost of similar engagements, such as field sales visits, contact center calls, and direct mail campaigns. Although not all business functions are optimal within a Social Media community, many organizations use Social Media communities to provide customer service by trained community members to other members at a lesser cost than other customer service venues, such as a contact center. Intuit and Microsoft are good examples of organizations that offer self-service Social Media communities. Communities can also be a cost-effective way to disseminate information to customers and prospects.

- **To achieve first-mover advantage**—Creating a Social Media community before competitors create a similar community gives an organization *first-mover advantage.* An organization with first-mover advantage is able to create a two-way dialogue and engage with customers and prospects prior to competitors offering a similar service. The Mobil SHC Club private Social Media community for lubrication engineers is a good example of the value of first-mover advantage.

- **To enhance internal collaboration**—Organizations are increasingly using Social Media communities to enhance internal collaboration among employees. This includes, for example, sharing internal knowledge, raising employee issues, and developing solutions to customer problems.

- **To increase customer knowledge**—If your organization offers products that are very technical, a Social Media community can be a good vehicle to facilitate the exchange of information. This includes both written materials available within the community (for example, technical data sheets) and exchanges between community members about community tools such as discussion forums.

- **To optimize the sales pipeline**—A Social Media community helps optimize the sales pipeline as customers participate in the community, reading customer comments about the organization's products and services before making a purchase decision.

- **To secure a regular flow of leads and new customers**—As part of the lead-generation process, a Social Media community provides a forum for prospects to learn more about the organization's products and services as well as to communicate with community members (both internal employees and external customers).

- **To minimize customer churn**—A Social Media Community can assist in minimizing customer churn—that is, help secure customer retention—by keeping current customers engaged and providing a forum for customer service and customer comments.

- **To expand distribution channels**—A Social Media community can be an effective channel for communicating with an organization's distributors and partners (for example, using the community collaboratively to provide and manage sales leads).

- **To drive product innovation**—Social Media communities are often used to drive product innovation through community tools such as ideation and crowdsourcing. For example, IBM uses its own internal community to enhance product innovation by enabling IBM staff to make recommendations within the community on how to better engage customers with new products. Innovation resulting from IBM's Social Media community efforts has been extraordinarily successful.

## Leveraging Private Social Media Communities to Achieve Social CRM Success

In Chapter 3, "Social Media Pilot Case Study," I described a five-step process that Front Runner used to create its private Social Media community plan and integrate social insight from the community into the Social CRM application:

1. Constituent Selection
2. Technographic Profiling
3. Business Goal Identification and Community Metrics
4. Vendor Selection
5. Community Engagement Plan

We'll now dig deeper into the first two of these steps, along with community metrics, as well as look at other requirements for creating a successful private Social Media community that is a requisite for a successful Social CRM.

### Constituent Selection and Technographic Profiling

Social Media is a new way for organizations to communicate with employees, consumers, partners, and other stakeholders. For organizations to succeed in their Social Media initiative, they need to be careful to understand their community's target audience. Here are two important questions to ask:

1. What purpose will the Social Media community serve for community members (for example, entertainment, knowledge, connection, commerce, influence, or other)?

2. What do the targeted members care about? Best practices suggest the members of the most successful communities expect to find three value-adds:

   - **Interaction**—The ability to connect with the organization, along with the ability to communicate with other people who have similar interests, trying to find similar solutions to similar problems.

   - **Access**—Access to SMEs who really understand the problems that other audience members are trying to solve.

   - **Deals**—Members can get member-only discounts and specific deals before they become available to the general public.

An organization will increase its success for an external Social Media community if it encompasses an audience with which the company is already communicating (for example, customers, distribution channel partners, or employees). Typically the largest audience group for a private Social Media community will be the organization's clients. Verizon FIOS's community encourages an FIOS customer with an issue to visit the Verizon FIOS private community to obtain support from other Verizon FIOS users on the issue.

The second largest audience group for an external private community is prospects. Sephora's private community has a tremendous amount of engagement with prospects concerning its makeup and skin care products. The third largest audience group for an external private community will be distributors and partners. As noted in Chapter 2, private communities can provide access to important information and provide a forum for communications between different distributors and partners. Volvo Construction Equipment division has done an admirable job using its community to create a two-way dialogue with business partners and customers.

Organizations need to spend time in advance carefully selecting their constituent audience prior to performing appropriate technographic profiling for potential members (remember that technographic profiles concern Internet-related demographics, such as the websites members or prospects visit, how actively they participate in public and private Social Media communities, how frequently they blog, and so on). To secure community members, an organization should look at existing distribution lists of people who receive its newsletter as well as for people who have opted in to receive information from the organization or have participated in other organizational events or asked staff for more information about the organization's products and services. Once the community is up and running, the organization should share with targeted members and prospects the community's accomplishments—including contest and poll results, the latest blogs and forum discussions, and so on—to drive additional traffic to the community.

## Community Governance

The governance structure and the qualified personnel staffing it comprise another critical component for a successful community that is often overlooked. Here are the typical high-level governance roles that must be established by an organization for a Social Media community project:

- **Project sponsor**—Owns the community at the highest level and oversees the community's objectives, links to corporate strategy, budget, and metrics. This is the Social Media community evangelist who will sell the community concept to the rest of the executive team.

- **Steering committee**—This committee comprises the managerial group involved in the community. It sets policies and procedures as well as approves content topics and project schedules.

- **Community manager**—This individual owns the community at a tactical level and creates guidelines and manages issues associated with the community.

- **Community moderator**—This individual (or individuals) enforces community guidelines while monitoring and raising issues for resolution. The community moderator makes sure that issues raised in the Social Media community are responded to in a timely matter. If no solution is readily available, the community moderator acknowledges that an issue was raised and promises to deliver a solution in a timely manner. Issues raised in the community should be responded to within 24 hours after they have been posted.

In addition to these high-level governance roles, every successful Social Media community has a carefully considered *community project team* comprising representatives from every group in the organization affected by the Social Media Community project. A word of caution: Each project team will differ somewhat based on the goals of the community, the issues being raised in the community, and the audience being targeted by the community. Moreover, depending on the size of the community, some people may have more than one role.

Here's a list of the typical internal team members:

- HR
- Corporate communications
- IT
- Marketing
- Sales
- Product management
- Product development
- Legal

External team members include the following:

- Community customer service personnel
- Legal advisors
- IT advisors
- Alliances/partners
- Branding, PR, and monitoring agencies
- Compliance advisors

Last, here's a list of roles typically found in the community deployment team:

- Project sponsor
- Project manager
- Project team
- Community manager
- Community moderator
- Editorial/content manager

- Bloggers/content providers
- Technical support
- Web/graphic support
- Public affairs and PR support

Social Media communities have a variety of Social Media tools that can be used to build the community. These tools include the following:

- Blogs
- Forums
- Idea sharing
- Ratings
- Polls
- Contests
- Offers
- Photos
- Video/TV
- Podcasts, RSS, widgets, and so on

I will comment specifically on the importance of SMEs and blogs, but each of these tools helps to drive member engagement in the community by providing members with product and industry information, the latest research, subject matter expertise (internal and external), and partner and customer input.

### Subject Matter Experts

Each Social Media community must have its own personality. Creating the right personality for a community has a lot to do with the audience it serves. For example, a technology organization's Social Media community's personality will be technical, with many technology-related blogs. A B2B industrial community's personality will be professional, with lots of input from SMEs. A B2C entertainment organization community's personality will be a "fun" community (for example, Disney's Social Media community).

SMEs play an important role in establishing the personality of the community. Considerable care must to be taken to secure the right SMEs for each community. As an example, in one of AAA's B2C Social Media communities that ISM helped design and build, one of the big attractions is the "Ask Pete" feature, where SME Pete (an AAA employee) encourages community members to post car questions that he then answers. Pete is a fun fellow, and his answers are always amusing. A word of caution: Organizations should be careful about removing the personal voice of the SME and replacing it with standard corporate responses. Doing so can damage a community, given the SME's impact on the community's personality.

## Blogs

Think of a blog as an organization's branded newspaper or journal. Blogs support marketing by providing news about the brand ("Did you know about..."). They also support customer service by identifying issues and providing product tips ("Do you need help with..." and "Did you know that..."), and they support innovation by helping to improve products ("You can make your life better by..."). The key components of a successful blog include a one-to-many outreach, frequent updates, the ability to comment and respond, and the inclusion of text and rich media (hyperlinks, images, and video).

Key blog benefits include the following:

- **Targeted voices**—Human voices that customers can relate to, speaking to customers in "their" language.
- **Responsiveness**—Evidence the organization listens and does not just talk. A blog is a platform from which the organization can respond quickly to events.
- **Thought leadership**—A human face to the brand; a platform to engage influencers.
- **Interactivity**—The blog is a destination site, not a billboard. In addition, interactivity can improve search ranking.

The organization must also make a decision about whether to use individual or group blogs. Neither one is inherently better than the other. With individual blogs, customers can build closer relationships with the blogger, but the blogger needs to provide very frequent content updates. Group blogs distribute the content load and offer a wider range of expertise, but it is critical to have a central focus and personality on the group blog to engage community members. Regardless of whether an organization uses individual or group blogs, it is important that the organization create and adhere to a blog calendar schedule, thus avoiding long gaps between posts, which can be damaging to the community.

Some of the common mistakes that organizations make in their blog effort include the following:

- Using a ghost blog, fake blog, or fake blog comments
- Using fictitious characters as blog authors
- Heavy-handed moderation
- Being too formal and polished
- Regurgitating existing organizational collateral
- Not using blog editorial calendar
- Long gaps between blog posts
- Sending blog posts through PR and marketing for rewriting
- Having a complicated blog approval process that impacts the blog's freshness

### Community Guidelines and Community Moderation

Three types of Social Media guidelines must be put into place to ensure a successful community:

- Documented and concise community guidelines to ensure that the tone within the community is positive and productive for all community members. Think of community guidelines as the rules of engagement for all members to "play nice" within the community. All members joining a community must agree to the guidelines prior to being added. These guidelines should contain explicit terms regarding what can and cannot be done within the community (no use of profanity, no overt selling or pitching of products and services, and so on).
- An accessible privacy policy that clearly describes how the organization will protect community data from unauthorized use.
- Written employee guidelines that spell out the rules for engagement in a community by internal employees (for example, they get "badged" as company employees).

Social Media community moderation is also a key success factor—and too often the downfall of a community. Nobody likes to go to a community that has little activity and lots of old posts and materials. The community moderator oversees all posts in accordance with the community guidelines. Positive moderation rewards engagement and encourages members to participate in the community. The moderator is also responsible for leveraging the moderation tools contained in most Social Media community technology platforms. These include pre-moderation tools (only approved content will appear in the community), user-generated alerts, notifications of posts, filters for profanity and watchwords, and a moderator board for documentation of community guideline enforcement. The moderator should also have the ability to send private messages to each community member (for example, "I find your last few posts inappropriate and in violation of community guidelines for these reasons") as well as the ability to create and manage multiple member ranks, badges, and roles.

## Social Media Community Metrics

Again, it is very important that community metrics are set at the outset of the community initiative. It is very difficult to report on Social Media community success if success metrics have not been clearly defined early on. Community metrics typically include community health and business metrics.

### Community Health Metrics

These metrics are straightforward but take time to achieve. They measure member activity and engagement in the community.

- **Growth in participation**—Number of registered members, new members since inception of the community, followers, fans, and so on
- **Growth in content**—Number of posts attached to each blog or forum
- **Growth in traffic**—Page views
- **Responsiveness**—Amount of time between a post and the first reply
- **Topic interaction**—Number of posts per thread
- **Engagement**—Level of activity (for example, how often members visit the community and how long they stay)

*Business Metrics*

These metrics are more difficult to quantify but are equally important. Remember the Front Runner community metrics in Chapter 3: Increase sales by 0.5 percent by the end of the pilot, resulting from customer participation in the Social Media community. Sales lift will be determined by measuring sales growth of community members versus nonmembers. Here are several popular business metrics:

- Increased revenue
- Improved customer satisfaction and loyalty
- Cost avoidance or reduction (for example, how much was saved by using the community to respond to customer service issues rather than sending these issues to contact center personnel)
- Better products and services resulting from ideas generated in the community
- Higher brand recognition and related business-profile metrics

# Emerging Social Media Community Issue: Social Media Policies and Guidelines

Internal employees play an important role in helping to achieve successful communities. After all, who better knows the ins and outs of an organization's products and services than qualified employees? Yet, a 2012 Gartner study reports that 60 percent of employers are or are planning to monitor their employee use of Social Media participation.[1] A survey of 1,400 CIOs by Robert Half Technology reports that 54 percent of U.S. organizations ban workers from using Social Media sites on the job.[2] A DLA Piper study reports one-third of employers disciplined employees for Social Media postings.[3] However, the same study shows that 39 percent are using social technologies for employee communication and engagement, 42 percent for recruitment, and 28 percent for team working. An ISM survey found that 58 percent of survey respondents work at an organization without a Social Media policy in place.[4] All these statistics confirm that there is a large employee/employer divide when it comes to the use of Social Media communities. This divide has already attracted the attention of the National Labor Relations Board, which is taking a bigger role in defining when an employee can and cannot be fired for Social Media behavior.

My take: This issue needs to be resolved soon because monitoring—or even worse, banning—participation in Social Media communities flies in the face of Generation Y employees. More concerning, it can negatively impact the health of the organization's private Social Media community and, in turn, Social CRM efforts.

## Private Social Media Communities Case Studies

Let's review three companies' attempts to achieve meaningful Social CRM based on leveraging social insight from their private Social Media communities. Company A, a B2B2C, created a solid community business case that linked its community to its Social CRM system. The initiative was shot down by its executive team, which thought it would take too long to realize the proposed revenue gains.

Company B is a B2C. Its executive team clearly understood the value · of Social CRM and the need to create a private Social Media community that drives social insight directly into its Social CRM system's customer profiles. The team agreed on a sound financial metric—the percentage increase in sales from community members versus non-community members—and measured this on a quarterly basis. Company B allowed two years to achieve a self-sustaining community, which has been met. There was also a lot of time spent ensuring that meaningful customer comments made in the Social Media community could be easily harvested and sent to that customer's Social CRM customer profile, giving Company B's sales and marketing personnel deeper insight into each customer's needs. The organization's efforts have paid off in increased sales and customer loyalty.

Company C is a global B2B manufacturer. Given its dominant market position, new initiatives such as its private Social Media community receive careful scrutiny in a very structured approval process. This means that Company C's executives worldwide have had time to buy into and actively engage in the initiative. Its community business case linked the community to its global digital strategy, and included a meaningful ROI at the end of a two-year period. Although the company it has not yet integrated insights gathered from community members into customer profiles, this will hopefully happen soon.

All three companies set out on a solid course to achieve Social CRM success. Unlike Company A, companies B and C accepted that building a self-sustaining Social Media community cannot be accomplished over-night. They acknowledged that it takes time and careful planning to create Social CRM success, but that the rewards more than offset the wait.

## Key Social Media Community Success Factors

- Ensure that Social Media initiatives support business goals.
- Take the time to understand the audience the community will be serving.
- Define success with clear metrics.
- Do not hamstring the community with too much overhead, including the following:
  - Complex workflows
  - Heavy editing
  - Multilayer review process
  - Obvious corporate scrutiny
- Understand that successful communities are driven by the membership. Management should ask the community members what they are most interested in and make every effort to address stated interests.
- Develop a strong community voice.
- Monitor the community carefully, but do not try to control it.
- Be prepared to respond quickly to community input, both positive and negative. Comments from the organization should never be anonymous. If a community member is upset and posts a negative comment, it should be addressed positively and in accordance with the community guidelines that members have agreed to.
- Pick topics to discuss in the Social Media community that the organization and community members are passionate about.

Chapter 6, "Social Media Knowledge Communities and Social CRM," discusses the nuts and bolts of internal Social Media communities and collaboration tools as well as their integration with Social CRM.

# Endnotes

1. Garter, "Conduct Digital Surveillance Ethically and Legally: 2012 Update," http://www.gartner.com/newsroom/id/2028215 (March 29, 2012).

2. Robert Half Technology, "Whistle—But Don't Tweet—While You Work," http://rht.mediaroom.com/index.php?s=131&item=790 (October 6, 2009).

3. DLA Piper, "Shifting Landscapes: The Online Challenge to Traditional Business Models," http://viewer.zmags.com/publication/29f83ba6#/29f83ba6/1 (October 2011).

4. ISM survey conducted with 70 respondents on November 10, 2014, as part of a Social Media Policy webinar, 58% reporting working at a company without a social media policy in place.

# 6

## Social Media Knowledge Communities and Social CRM

Social Media is an effective tool to achieve meaningful enterprise collaboration (knowledge communities) as well as channel and partner collaboration. The Social CRM framework described in Chapter 4, "Leverage Social Media Information to Advance Your Social CRM Efforts," shows how an organization can monitor and filter relevant insight generated from Social Media communities, integrate it into the Social CRM application, and then leverage this information to better engage with customers (in this case, to better engage with internal employees and with channels/partners). This chapter explores this better engagement.

The administration of an organization's internal knowledge is also known as *knowledge management (KM)*. There is no consensus on the definition of KM. Ron Young, CEO/CKO at Knowledge Associates International, defines it as "the discipline of enabling individuals, teams and entire organizations to collectively and systematically create, share and apply knowledge, to better achieve their objectives." Lew Platt, ex-CEO of Hewlett-Packard, appraises KM's benefits in his statement: "If only HP knew what it knows, it would make three times more profit tomorrow." GlaxoSmithKline defines KM as "the capabilities by which communities within an organization capture the knowledge that is critical to them, constantly improve it and make it available in the most effective manner to those who need it, so that they can exploit it creatively to add value as a normal part of their work."

Social Media tools do an outstanding job of capturing information from business colleagues and channels/partners and then sharing this information collaboratively. Knowledge can originate anywhere in an organization, but when it is channeled and gathered into the Social Media platform's knowledgebase, it can then easily be shared among community participants.

## Why Knowledge Management Collaboration Is Growing in Importance

The severe economic recession that started with the 2008 stock market crash forced a lot of baby boomers to put off their retirement plans. Consequently, there is quite a large number of college graduates having problems finding suitable employment, in part because baby boomers are holding on to their jobs longer than expected. Here is an excellent explanation of this age-related impact on organizations as determined by Kathy Barton, Senior VP of Social CRM at ISM, Inc.:

> "There are many organizations with the workforce staff whose age is 45+ and new hires that are in their early working years (20s to early 30s). There is an age gap as there is no intermediate age group (late 30s to early 40s). As these older workers retire, there will be a problem of a loss of knowledge and experience for the organization."

One way of alleviating this loss of institutional memory is to create Social Media knowledge communities and open them to existing employees, ex-employees, and external channel/partners. Current knowledge-management practices tend to be static—noncollaborative and quickly dated—but Social Media knowledge communities are collaborative by nature and are continually updated by community members. Leveraging Social Media knowledge communities to share information means increased flexibility and easier collaboration. It also can mean a big savings for the organization.

McKinsey Global Institute did a study on the value of global collaboration in 2012. Based on the analysis of 4,200 organizations, it found that social technologies could add between $900 billion and $1.3 trillion to enterprise organizations' bottom line.[1] Two-thirds of this value comes from "improved communication within and across the enterprise." The internal use of Social Media as part of the knowledge-management process also increases the productivity of skilled workers by breaking down silos and leveraging expertise. There are often pockets of information within organizational silos that do not get shared with other silos unless there is an opportunity to share such information through methods such as Social Media.

## Painless Knowledge Management

Knowledge management capture tools are challenging to operationalize, but Social Media knowledge management communities are simple to use and very cost effective. To succeed at leveraging Social Media knowledge management communities, all employees must learn to move requests for expertise or problem solving from phone calls and emails to an internal and/or partner Social Media community. For example, if employee John typically sends an email to employee Mary asking for assistance solving a problem, it is a one-to-one conversation. Unless a structured information-sharing process has been put into place, any resolution to John's problem typically is not made available to other employees or partners. If Mary's proposed solution is captured in an internal or partner Social Media community, other employees or partners with proper user access rights to the community can now collaborate by discussing John's problem, by reviewing Mary's proposed solution, and possibly by brainstorming even better solutions.

This collaboration does not require approval of posted comments prior to being placed in the knowledge-management database. Furthermore, using standard Social Media community tools, enterprise expertise can be monitored and filtered so that only relevant information makes its way into the searchable database that is a part of the Social Media platform. Social Media communities typically are self-policed to confirm that all the posted information is correct. Over time, enterprise expertise can also be amended and corrected so that information accuracy improves (this is how Wikipedia works). The result of internal Social Media knowledge communities is powerfully improved institutional memory, resulting from the Social Media knowledge base created as a byproduct of employee/partner responses to questions posted by other employees/partners. Many employees/partners are accustomed to using Social Media communities to get restaurant or product reviews, and are typically pleased to participate in an internal Social Media knowledge community.

I know a global organization that has invited back several of its retired employees to contribute their specific skills and knowledge to the Social Media knowledge community. The organization pays the retirees an hourly wage to answer questions posted in the community and to share issue resolutions. It is an excellent, low-cost way to keep retired employees engaged while they add valuable knowledge to the organization's Social Media knowledgebase.

## Integrating Social Media Knowledge Communities and Social CRM

There are two integration points between Social Media knowledge communities and Social CRM:

- **Starting in the Social Media community**—A customer issue is identified, discussed, and possibly resolved in a Social Media knowledge community. It next is integrated into a customer or partner profile used for customer or partner engagement purposes. For example, one of ISM's customers manufactures parts for the automotive industry—a truly global industry. When this company has an issue with Ford in any part of the world, the issue is raised in the Ford Social Media knowledge community. Others from around the company who are members of the Ford Social Media knowledge community join in and offer their suggestions for resolving the Ford issue. This issue and its potential resolution, in turn, are integrated as a petal on the Ford global customer profile inside this company's Social CRM application. Thus, all company employees calling on Ford that have access to the Ford customer profile are knowledgeable about the Ford issue and potential resolution.

- **Starting in the Social CRM application**—Alternatively, if there is a problem or issue that has been noted in a petal of a customer or partner profile located within the Social CRM application (for example, in the customer service petal), it can be manually or automatically uploaded via workflow into the Social Media knowledge community for review and discussion. Community members then brainstorm a proposed solution for the customer or partner. The solution is then imported back into the profile and stored in the community database for use in solving similar problems or issues in the future.

# Knowledge Management Mini Case Study

Company A, a global, best-in-class manufacturer, sells its products via distributors, but several years ago came to realize the potential dangers of losing contact with the customers of these distributors, which Company A calls "consumers." Company A's challenge is to utilize Social CRM to maintain a two-way dialogue with the consumers while motivating distributors to participate in the private Social Media community created as the foundation to its Social CRM initiative.

To meet this objective, Company A has created (in addition to its public Facebook social community) a private social community with three separate "entry doors," as follows:

- **Entry Door 1**—Open to consumers who want to share their opinions and new product ideas with each other, and with Company A's employees who monitor the community.

- **Entry Door 2**—Open to Company A's distributors, where forums and blogs focus more on sharing best practices for distributors participating in the industry.

- **Entry Door 3**—The third door focuses on topics around efficiency in distribution, where both distributors and their consumers share ideas with one another.

Company A's private Social Media community is built on a Social Media platform that offers blogs, forums, contests, polls, Ask the Expert, site searches, product data sheets, and so on. In addition to leveraging these standard Social Media functions, Company A has now begun to focus on three related activities:

- To facilitate Door 3 activities (that is, the discussion of topics around efficiency in distribution), Company A has opted to leverage the knowledge database that comes with the Social Media platform. More specifically, in addition to distributors and consumers, Company A has opened the community to a limited group of Company A's retirees. Creative thoughts that are generated during the "efficiency in distribution" discussions are tagged and automatically stored in the Social Media platform's knowledge base.

- Company A is filtering and integrating social insights from the private community directly into the consumer profiles held in its Social CRM system. This allows Company A's customer-facing personnel to have a better and more complete picture of their consumers.

- Company A is coordinating and integrating Social Media activity with search engine optimization (SEO) in mind. Search is still a huge source for securing customers, but Social Media is growing in importance within search engines. Social content (for example, images, articles, video, and tweets) are links in organic search results. Therefore, organizations must take care of *what* and *how* they post Social Media blog entries, tweets, forums, and so on. In fact, recent studies confirm that consumers exposed to a brand's Social Media content are 2.8 times more likely to search on that brand's terms, that consumers exposed to a brand's Social Media content are 1.7 times more likely to search with the intention of making a purchase, and that, overall, brands report a 50 percent lift in click-through rates from consumers exposed to both Social Media and paid search.[2]

Company A's private Social Media community is a work in progress, but initial pilot-period metrics show a 12 percent lift in sales for consumers belonging to the community versus consumers who do not.

Next up in Chapter 7, "Overcoming Skepticism to Exploit Social CRM," I will describe the Social CRM success formula that can be used to bring about a fundamental shift in how an organization can interact with its customers and other organizations.

## Endnotes

1. McKinsey Global Institute, "The Social Economy: Unlocking Value and Productivity Through Social Technologies," http://www.mckinsey.com/insights/high_tech_telecoms_internet/the_social_economy (July 2012).

2. GroupM Search, "The Influenced: Social Media, Search and the Interplay of Consideration and Consumption," http://www.scribd.com/doc/20703026/The-Influenced-Social-Media-Search-and-the-Interplay-of-Consideration-and-Consumption#scribd (October 2009).

# 7

## Overcoming Skepticism to Exploit Social CRM

The previous three chapters describe a Social CRM framework, look into the value-add and requirements of external- and internal-facing Social Media communities, and make the strong link between Social Media communities and Social CRM. This chapter delves into why I think some executives are still hesitant to jump into Social CRM.

The Social CRM industry is a very robust market. MarketsandMarkets forecasts the worldwide market of $1.9 billion in 2013 growing to $9.1 billion in 2018.[1] This represents a compound annual growth rate of 36.5 percent during this five-year period. The following factors account for this impressive, continuing growth:

- The rising focus on creating meaningful customer engagement
- The continuing need to better understand customers' sentiments
- Acknowledgement of customers' strong desire for two way dialogue with the companies they want to buy from
- The explosion of Social Media platforms that easily deliver the capability for that two-way dialogue
- Recognition that collaborating in real time helps management at all levels to make more informed decisions

Organizations are now placing increased emphasis on listening to their customers in Social Media communities because of Social CRM's value-add. The Social CRM framework described in Chapter 4, "Leverage Social Media Information to Advance Your Social CRM Efforts," shows how Social CRM gathers social insight from both public and private social communities, filters this free-form information to ensure that organizations have captured meaningful social insights, and then integrates this filtered insight into Social CRM customer profiles to provide a deeper understanding of the organizations' customers and prospects. With Social CRM, organizations can now leverage all the transactional information that exists in their Social CRM system (for example, sales forecasts, customer service incident management, and market campaigns) *in addition to* sentiment-based insight gathered from Social Media communities, including how customers feel about doing business with these organizations.

In the 30 years of my industry involvement, I have never witnessed the amount of confusion about and skepticism of when and how best to adopt a new CRM-related process/toolset as I have with Social CRM. At the same time, organizations that have stopped questioning and have charged forward with Social CRM are beginning to pull away from their competitors.

One of the benefits of working with global, best-in-class organizations during the years is that these organizations have the resources to try new ideas early on. My work with the American Automobile Association (AAA) clubs is a case in point. Chapter 1, "Social CRM: The Intersection of Social Media and CRM," describes how ISM assisted multiple AAA clubs to set up private Social Media communities and how some of the clubs harvest valuable member information and place this information directly into each member's customer profile. As a result, AAA frontline personnel in several clubs are better positioned to serve their members because they have a deeper insight onto their members' needs, along with a better read on how well members think AAA can meet their individual needs. But despite the strong concepts behind Social CRM, many organizations harbor a good deal of skepticism of it. Executives tend to shy away from opening organizations to a healthy, two-way customer exchange. Typically, executives voice the following types of concerns:

- What if the customer says malicious things about us?
- What if a disgruntled customer goes viral on us?
- How much resource commitment is required to do Social CRM right?
- Why fix what is not broken or change the formula now? The organization has been very successful to date.

# A Social CRM Success Formula

I encourage hard-core skeptics to jump ahead to Part VII, "The Future of Social CRM," to read about where Social CRM is headed over the next decade. After you do, I ask, does it still make sense for your organization to stand on the sidelines during this fundamental shift in the way customer and organizations interact with one another?

To skeptics who remain open to discussion, I point to the fact that Social Media communities (the core of every successful Social CRM strategy) have become the number-one interactive source for buyers. I also note that more than 80 percent of Internet consumers search online for organization/product information, trusting peer-generated content more than organizational or professional insight. The Social Media revolution isn't going away, and executives need not fear change. I recommend taking a proactive approach to learning more about Social CRM. Here is a measured, four-step approach to exploiting Social CRM benefits:

1. Take the time and invest in listening to customers. There are dozens of cost-effective ways to monitor what customers are saying about the organization.
2. Build a simple Social Media community to attract customers and prospects and open a two-way dialogue.
3. Be sure to integrate customer Social Media insight directly into the organization's Social CRM system so that all frontline personnel who have access rights gain a 360-degree view of the customer.
4. Leverage new Social CRM processes and tools in sales, marketing, customer service, ebusiness, and analytics to help drive new product/service sales.

The following is a short Social CRM success story to illustrate these benefits. The customer is a global leader in food manufacturing that has a growing foodservice division. Until recently this division relied heavily on the well-established food distribution channel to sell to and service its customers. The organization got a wake-up call when economic times got tough and distributors began to offer their own competitive products. Although respectful of the key role that the well-established distribution channel played, the food manufacturer decided to focus its attention on enhancing a two-way dialogue with the end customers—not solely with restaurant owners that the distributors sold to, but also with chefs that work in specific restaurants. The company built social communities that discuss food preparation, held chef contests, shared food trends, polled end users about new ideas, and so on.

The results generated by the food manufacturer's social community have been impressive. End users are now "pulling" the company's products through the distribution channel, driving new growth. The company can now quickly uncover A-list customers worthy of direct sales force visits. Sales and marketing processes are now more closely linked. The company also has begun to leverage customer insights to deliver new and highly profitable products.

Many organizations, including several global, best-in-class customers, are well on their way to mastering Social CRM to deliver increased customer satisfaction, loyalty, customer advocacy, and a meaningful ROI. Here's a response to the concerns raised previously that executives typically voice:

### Q: What if the customer says malicious things about us?

**A:** Customers do and will continue to say good and bad things about an organization on Social Media communities. Sharing stories positive and negative is what people do, and today's simple-to-use Social Media communities provide an ideal format for it. So, the question becomes, do you want to participate in this story sharing and be aware of what people are saying, or do you want to stick your head in the sand and hope for the best?

### Q: What if a disgruntled customer goes viral on us?

**A:** This is a potentially serious risk, but there are meaningful ways to mitigate it. I work with one of the world's largest manufacturers, which is very conservative and very careful about managing risk. Its track record is commendable. When it built its first Social Media community, it was careful to put in place a number of checks and balances to ensure that a disgruntled customer would not go viral.

First, the company opted for a private versus a public Social Media community because it would have control over who joined the community and what was being said on it. Second, potential community members were carefully vetted prior to being invited into the community, and each new member had to agree to strict community guidelines before being allowed to join. Third, the community is carefully monitored—issues that concern moderators rise quickly through a structured process to business owners and legal counsel for swift advice and action.

There have been no disgruntled customers in the community. Summing up, the organization determined that the risk of not participating in the digital revolution—in this case, through the creation of private Social Media communities—far outweighed the risk of a potential disgruntled customer going viral, a risk that the organization proactively mitigates daily.

### Q: How much resource commitment is required to do Social CRM right?

**A:** This is a fair, valuable question. The answer depends in part on whether the organization wants to do all the work in-house or whether it is open to using external resources; whether the Social Media community and/or Social CRM initiative is domestic or global (the latter adds new challenges—language, data privacy, and fit); and how tightly the organization intends to integrate social insight into the Social CRM application.

Here are some high-level guidelines that should be adjusted case by case:

- For a medium-size domestic Social CRM initiative, one full-time employee plus two to three part-time internal and/or external resources will be required.

- For a large, global Social CRM initiative, two full-time employees plus four to six part-time internal and/or external resources will be required.

### Q: Why fix what is not broken or change the formula now? The organization has been very successful to date.

**A:** Many businesses have been impacted—or have gone away—as a result of Internet-based initiatives, including Social Media communities and Social CRM. No organization can run the risk of going the route that the book, travel agency, and music industries have been forced to follow, given the rapidly changing distribution channels and the availability of new tools to create two-way dialogues between manufacturers and consumers. A horse and buggy was a fine means of transportation into the early twentieth century, but buggy manufacturers forgot that they were in the transportation business, not the buggy-manufacturing business, as the automobile became the vehicle of choice.

## Social CRM Lessons Learned

Outcomes have been overwhelmingly positive for AAA, for the global food manufacturer, and all the other organizations that ISM has had the pleasure to work with on Social Media communities and Social CRM. Social CRM is the way of the future: It takes CRM to an entirely new level in terms of understanding customers, and it deepens a company's relationship with its customers.

Of the remaining Social CRM skeptics, I ask that you reflect on what Cisco CEO John Chambers said some years ago: "This collaboration that kids got through social networking is the future of business." To that I add, "Can the organization really wait much longer to successfully create and implement of its own Social CRM strategy?"

Part III, "Readying for Social CRM Implementation," initially looks at getting your Social CRM strategy right and selecting the right Social CRM software. Discussion will then turn to the all-important "people/process/technology" mix required for successful for Social CRM.

## Endnotes

1. MarketsandMarkets, "Customer Relationship Management (CRM) Market & Social CRM (Social Monitoring; Social Listening; Social Mapping; Social Measurements; Social Engagement; Social Middleware) – Global Advancements, Forecasts & Analysis (2013 – 2018)," May 2013.Social CRM: The Intersection of Social Media and CRM

# Part III
## Readying for Social CRM Implementation

# 8

## Getting Your Social CRM Strategy Right

Organizations often embark on a Social CRM initiative without having a clear vision of where they want to go and how they intend to get there. These organizations are the ones that end up reporting that their Social CRM implementation results are below user expectations. By now, this should not come as a surprise.

There are organizations, on the other hand, that take the time to properly define a Social CRM vision and use a structured methodology to create and realize their Social CRM strategy and implementation road map. Not surprisingly, these organizations tend to be ones that report implementation results that exceed user expectations.

A Social CRM strategy takes into account the business direction of the organization and how Social CRM will help the organization achieve this business strategy, and it includes a Social CRM road map to make all this happen. The following is a 12-step process for creating any organization's Social CRM strategy. Perhaps the organization has already taken one or more of these steps. Nonetheless, because these steps are designed to fit together like pieces in a puzzle, you should use the steps as a checklist to ensure that each step has been properly addressed before moving forward with the Social CRM initiative.

I foresee that most organizations' "Social" CRM strategy will remain a subset of their overall CRM strategy and implementation road map. This implies a tight integration of Social CRM with traditional CRM applications (for example, the integration of information stored in the Social CRM knowledgebase into customer profiles, and other CRM functions such as customer service, multichannel campaign management, sales force automation, and other back-office applications that may be integrated into the organization's comprehensive CRM system).

Relevant social insight information gathered from Social Media communities will be filtered using social monitoring tools and exported into the organization's Social CRM system. When engaging with the customer, users of the system will now have access to both incoming social insight information and information coming from other customer/prospect touchpoints (for example, in-person conversations, phone calls, emails, and surveys). This 12-step process focuses on Social CRM strategy, but much of the process can be applied for an organization's overall CRM strategy. (For more information on getting your CRM strategy right, please check out my book *CRM in Real Time*.)

## Step 1: Prepare an Executive Social CRM Vision

Gaining the support of the top management team is critical to driving the success of any Social CRM initiative. One way to accomplish this is to spend between 30 and 60 minutes with each of the business leaders from the organization's customer-facing departments, along with the CEO and other executives, such as the CIO, CMO, CSO and/or CFO, to discuss their Social CRM vision.

For example, one of the world's leading pharmaceutical companies contracted with ISM to formulate its Social CRM vision. It was clear that the CEO had given some thought to what Social CRM would mean for the company. He informed me that regardless of how customers contacted the company, he wanted them to receive outstanding service, and he was sure that Social CRM could help provide the tools to make this happen. When asked how he thought Social Media information filtering fit into his Social CRM vision, the CEO was less sure.

I next met with the business leaders of each of the firm's customer-facing departments. Surprisingly, each of these seven executives had a different view of what Social CRM was and what its primary objective would be for the company. Some of these executives understood that customer service issues could be tweeted, identified by a monitoring tool, downloaded into a customer service application (such as Salesforce.com) where a response could be formulated, and sent back out to the customer also via Twitter. Yet none of them had thought through, as the CEO had, how customer service would become a clear differentiator against the competition.

After formulating a Social CRM vision statement based on input received from all the interviewees, I arranged a Social CRM vision meeting with the CEO, the business leaders of customer-facing departments, and other executives, including the CIO and the CFO. The session's objective was to describe the wide-ranging Social CRM visions that had surfaced in the interviews so that, eventually, the group could agree on a definition for a unified Social CRM vision.

After considerable discussion and group facilitation, the group finally agreed to the following:

> *Understand, anticipate, and respond to the needs of existing and potential customers by leveraging social data to create stronger, mutually beneficial relationships. To meet this goal we must provide customer-facing personnel with relevant Social CRM tools (e.g., platforms, social analysis, sentiment analysis, etc.) that will help create/provide world-class customer service that will drive customer delight, loyalty, service differentiation, and long-term profitability.*

The definition is a bit too long, but the company gained a shared view of why Social CRM would be implemented. The significance of this Social CRM vision was reinforced when the top management team published its vision statement and distributed it to all personnel.

## Step 2: Determine Social CRM Business Requirements

In the case of the global pharmaceutical company, the goal was to uncover business requirements that impact the current day-to-day customer service operations. To uncover business requirements, you should set up additional 30-to-60-minute interviews with at least a dozen frontline personnel who work with customers all the time. Some organizations use a structured brainstorming session for eight to 12 frontline personnel to uncover business requirements. I have found it useful to invite one or more Social CRM vendors to show frontline personnel the "art of the possible" using Social CRM, so that when asked what would they like to see in the Social CRM initiative, they can brainstorm with an open mind. Using an external facilitator to manage the brainstorming session is a good way to ensure impartiality.

Write an interim business requirements report that summarizes and groups the findings by business function areas—whether it is sales, marketing, or customer service. Next, build user support for the Social CRM initiative by sharing the report with many additional frontline personnel to secure their feedback. Do the findings address the burning issues that frontline personnel face day to day? Are there additional requirements that need to be added to the list? Consider using an online survey to secure this input. It is easy to create and administer, and it allows many frontline personnel to feel that they are being heard. Once necessary alterations have been made, the business requirements report now becomes the "final" version.

Every organization must assess the business value of Social Media as a part of its business-requirements-gathering process. Social Media should be seen as another channel that will help the organization meet its broader strategic goals. Mapping how Social Media activities will support the organization's strategy is an important to-do in this step: Social Media conversations that are analyzed using Social Media monitoring and filtering tools will be placed into the organization's Social CRM system for customer engagement purposes.

A Social CRM program should identify which customers/prospects are talking about the organization's brands, which Social Media communities they are doing their talking on, which keywords must to be monitored, and so on. Fortunately most Social Media monitoring tools have built-in capabilities to identify these "who, what, and where" with ease. A Social CRM program also will require that all organizational stakeholders have the right tools and training to better manage the customer engagement process.

The idea behind this business requirement step is to be able to determine which Social CRM functionality will be realized in each of the three or four phases that typically get built out in a successful Social CRM initiative, with each typically coming three to six months apart. A reasonable Social CRM strategy would look similar to Table 8.1.

**Table 8.1** A Reasonable Social CRM Strategy

|  | Phase 1 Implementation | Phase 2 Implementation | Phase 3 Implementation | Phase 4 Implementation |
|---|---|---|---|---|
| Fulfillment of High-Priority Business Function Requirements | 80% | 60% | 40% | 20% |
| Fulfillment of Social CRM Vision Requirement | 20% | 40% | 60% | 80% |

The first phase of implementing the initiative would involve placing 80 percent of the emphasis on addressing the fulfillment of high-priority business functional requirements and 20 percent on achieving the orga-nization's agreed-on Social CRM vision. The second phase of the initia-tive, which is implemented three to six months after the first phase is completed, would place 60 percent of the emphasis on the fulfillment of high-priority business functional requirements and 40 percent on achiev-ing the organization's agreed-on Social CRM vision. In the third phase, the emphasis would shift to 40 percent on the fulfillment of high-priority business functional requirements and 60 percent on achieving the orga-nization's agreed-on Social CRM vision. In the fourth phase, 20 percent of the emphasis would be placed on the fulfillment of high-priority busi-ness functional requirements and 80 percent on achieving the organiza-tion's agreed-on Social CRM vision. By following this sequence, a more strategic Social CRM vision will eventually be accomplished as high-priority tactical business requirements—very important to frontline per-sonnel in the short term—are accomplished along the way. This multi-phase approach is a best practice and is by far the best way to secure buy-in from frontline personnel.

## Step 3: Identify Social CRM Technology Opportunities/Challenges

Successful Social CRM occurs when the people, process, and tech-nology are carefully mixed throughout the Social CRM initiative. The success of a Social CRM initiative depends on the following formula: People account for about 50 percent, process accounts for about 30 percent, and technology accounts for about 20 percent. So why identify Social CRM technology opportunities as a separate step when formulat-ing Social CRM strategy?

In Step 3, the organization will want to review current Social CRM technology trends and share these with the business leaders of customer-facing units. Although business-driven requirements should determine the Social CRM software that will be used, it is worthwhile to nonethe-less learn what, if any, technology trends may be of use to the organi-zation's strategy going forward. Invite the CEO and other executives, if possible, to discuss these trends. Be prepared: The purpose of the meeting is to demonstrate Social CRM technology trends and opportu-nities, and to have customer-facing personnel determine whether these trends will have a small, moderate, or large impact on their businesses. During this meeting, discuss any key technology issues relevant to the organization—whether they be skeletons in the closet (for example, low technology adoption issues) or simply other, ongoing technology projects that will need to be carefully integrated with the Social CRM initiative. Document the results of the meeting.

Steps 1, 2, and 3 of Social CRM strategy formulation—creating a Social CRM vision, determining business requirements, and identifying Social CRM technology opportunities/issues—need to be carefully coordinated to ensure that the Social CRM strategy formulation starts off on the right foot. Although an agreed-on vision is critical, it needs to be balanced with pragmatic business requirements over the short, medium, and long term. Unless known Social CRM technology trends are discussed, their potential impact may never be realized in the vision or as a way to fulfill identified business requirements. Take the time upon completion of Step 3 to ensure that each of the first three steps has been accomplished with excellence and that these three steps are in synch with one another.

## Step 4: Determine Key People Issues

This step identifies the people issues that are likely to impact a Social CRM initiative. The issues, which emerge from interviews conducted in Steps 1 and 2, include skepticism arising from issues such as past failed CRM-related efforts, a lack of a comprehensive training capability for frontline personnel, a corporate culture that does not promote information-sharing across customer-facing departments, failure to give Social CRM users the necessary time to learn how to utilize new social processes, and so on.

Once these issues are identified, the Social CRM strategy should include recommendations on how to overcome each one. Recommendations may include a comprehensive communications program to overcome initial skepticism and a detailed training program to address the need for multiple types of training (for everything from Social Media literacy, to effectively using new Social CRM processes and applications, to a revised information-sharing approach that actively encourages people to share Social Media information across customer-facing departments).

People issues have always been and will forever be the reason why a Social CRM initiative succeeds or fail. Do not underestimate their importance.

# Step 5: Develop a Long-Term Technical Road Map

Once business requirements have been determined (Step 2), the organization is ready to do a technology-gap analysis. The organization's executives will review what Social CRM technologies will be needed to support the identified business requirements and then compare these technologies to the existing technologies available to support the identified business requirements. The difference between what is needed and what is available at that time is called the *technology gap*. The gap may require additional hardware, software, and/or services, but it must be closed for the Social CRM system to deliver the identified business requirements.

To determine what technologies will be needed, the organization's technology SMEs associated with the Social CRM project team typically conduct research regarding, for example, Social Media platforms required to deliver identified business requirements, including available toolsets as well as their integration with Social CRM applications.

The organization next looks across all its technology projects, including the Social CRM project, to ensure that the desired Social CRM technology platform will be compatible with the technical architecture in place for all technology projects. The goal is to avoid technology "islands" that will cause unnecessary headaches over the longer term. Many options are available to determine an appropriate long-term technical architecture plan, including conducting one or more "grease-board" sessions. The end result is a technology road map that will provide appropriate guidance throughout the Social CRM implementation. Be sure to document the technology road map, including an agreed-on timetable for its implementation.

# Step 6: Identify Business Process Issues

Conduct cross-functional business process meetings for each customer-facing business area to identify and document key Social CRM business processes in the areas of sales, marketing, and customer service. Remember that Social CRM also has a set of business processes of its own—for example, how and when to perform Social Media community monitoring, how best to filter information coming from the monitoring activities, and what is the optimal way to integrate social insight into the organization's Social CRM application. Therefore, be sure to ask, "How will the organization utilize social insight coming from Social Media communities and what will be the impact on each identified sales, marketing, and customer service business process?" Assess each Social CRM process in terms of the seven business process success criteria: ownership, goals, metrics, interfaces, documentation, integrity, and fit with business vision. This will help ensure that selected business processes are ready for prime time. Finally, document the findings.

An observation: I find that highly complex processes with significant issues are inherently more difficult to change than simpler processes. Process enhancement can be challenging, so do not take on too much process change at any one time. Unless a process is completely broken or is entirely new, assess and enhance existing processes every 90 days and make small improvements on a continual basis.

## Step 7: Determine Customer Desires and Impact on Customers

In Social CRM, given that the organization is trying to create a two-way dialogue with customers, it becomes very important to receive regular feedback from them throughout the initiative. What if the customers don't see the value in the Social CRM business functions being proposed?

To ensure Social CRM success and to achieve a meaningful two-way dialogue with customers, follow these steps to reinforce the importance of gathering valuable customer input throughout the Social CRM initiative:

- Work with customers to understand their Social CRM needs; focus groups, customer questionnaires, and online surveys are effective ways to gather customer input.
- Seek out and listen carefully to customer feedback regarding planned Social CRM functionality.
- Based on customer input, determine which Social Media communities are well suited for inclusion in the organization's Social CRM strategy.
- Work with both the organization's customer-facing personnel and customers to determine the most appropriate way to secure needed customer information.

In addition, remember to do the following:

- Document all customer input and findings.
- Allow key organizational personnel time to learn how to effectively use all necessary Social Media communication platforms (Twitter, Facebook, LinkedIn, Google+, and whatever is invented in the future).
- Keep in mind that Social CRM will need to work on the most-used mobile devices and tablets as their usage increases.

## Step 8: Determine Social CRM Competitive Alternatives and Metrics

An organization can become overly proud of its Social CRM strategy and can assume that existing customers and prospects are eagerly awaiting the rollout. To ensure that customers will accept and adopt the new Social CRM strategy, the organization should perform a competitive Social CRM analysis. Find out what competitive applications are available to customers in the marketplace. Make sure the Social CRM offering is as good as or better than the competition's. If this is not the case, return to Step 1 in this 12-step process.

An organization must define Social CRM metrics at the outset of the initiative, and these must be tracked regularly (I like to track metrics monthly). Traditional CRM metrics such as opportunity close ratios, email offer click-through rates, and first call resolution time are good metrics, but in a Social CRM initiative special attention should also be paid to social sentiment measures such as social reach, advocacy, and perceived value.

## Step 9: Provide Social CRM Program Observations and Recommendations

Prepare and deliver a formal Social CRM program observations and recommendations document that includes the Social CRM vision, identifies Social CRM business requirements and customer inputs, and highlights people, process, and technology issues that will impact the successful implementation of the Social CRM initiative. Present these observations and recommendations to the executive team and to the business leaders of customer-facing departments for comment and approval.

## Step 10: Create a Social CRM Road Map

Once the Social CRM document from Step 9 has been approved, the organization is ready to create a Social CRM road map. This road map is a critical step in pulling together several inputs that will have an impact on the overall success of the organization's initiative. These inputs include other complementary and competitive corporate initiatives, IT initiatives, other business initiatives, Social CRM prerequisites, and Social CRM business functionality and technical features. Chart these inputs on a three-year quarterly log, and be sure to identify dependencies among relevant initiatives. In addition to helping ensure the initiative's success, the Social CRM road map also serves as a document that is discussed with stakeholders in regard to how the Social CRM initiative fits into all other ongoing and planned corporate initiatives.

## Step 11: Recommend a Social CRM Program Management Approach

This step offers suggestions for implementing the recommended Social CRM strategy and resulting Social CRM road map. It typically includes project management office (PMO) recommendations/policies/ procedures, organization design (including a project governance structure), and project roles and responsibilities.

## Step 12: Prepare the Social CRM Program Business Case

The business case is the document that most organizations use to approve the Social CRM investment. The Social CRM program business case should consist of these five parts:

- Executive summary. This is an overview of what happens when, to whom, and at what cost.
- Financials. This includes specific value proposition and ROI information.
- Key risks and mitigating factors.
- Operational/organizational impact issues.
- Appendixes that detail the basis of the value proposition.

The 12-step Social CRM strategy formulation process is illustrated in Figure 8.1. Again, the 12 steps comprise a checklist of requirements for creating a successful Social CRM strategy implementation road map.

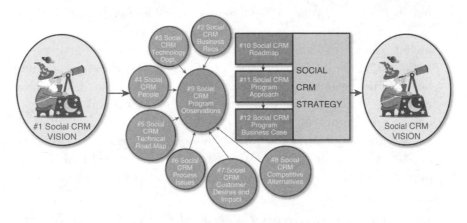

**Figure 8.1** The 12-step Social CRM strategy formulation process

In Chapter 9, "Social CRM Software Selection and Vendor Negotiation," I examine the process for selecting an appropriate Social CRM software vendor and negotiating the best deal with that vendor.

# 9

## Social CRM Software Selection and Vendor Negotiation

Once the organization has completed its Social CRM strategy, it will be necessary to select a Social CRM software application. In addition to standard CRM sales, marketing, customer service, and business analytics, functionality will also leverage social insight coming from public and private Social Media communities in order for the organization to better engage with customers. Software selection requires that the prioritized business functional requirements be gathered and that the desired technical features be identified. This implies that executives and frontline personnel from sales, marketing, customer service, and other departments are working together to ensure that their business and integration needs are understood prior to embarking on the software selection process.

## How to Select Software

Luckily, several excellent Social CRM software selection methodologies exist to help organizations get the process started. Here is a ten-step methodology that I developed and that many organizations have implemented over the years with reasonable success.

### Step 1: Technical Baseline Review

The organization's technical staff must define the current technical platform and capabilities in place. This includes current hardware and software, data synchronization tools, current/planned links to Social Media communities, and Social Media monitoring tools.

### Step 2: Customer Visits with the Customer-Facing Personnel

A Social CRM project team member should talk to a cross-section of customer-facing representatives from sales, marketing, customer service, and partners, as appropriate. The objective is to observe what technology and business processes they use in their day-to-day tasks, what works and what does not, how they resolve customer issues that come up, and so on. Anywhere from a half-day to a full day per representative should be allotted. Observations from the visits will serve as input for the brainstorming session and the needs-analysis questionnaires.

### Step 3: Brainstorming Session

Conduct a structured session with key personnel, including sales representatives, marketing and sales managers, executives, customer service managers, and IT specialists to discuss their perceived Social CRM business-functional needs. Typically this is a two- to four-hour session for eight to 12 people (in a global project this can extend to 12 to 16 people). These participants are typically chosen as the superuser group to participate in other steps noted later on in this methodology. Superusers act as ambassadors of the Social CRM initiative, so they must be picked with care. It is useful to invite in one or more Social CRM vendors the day before the brainstorming session to show superusers the "art of the possible" using Social CRM, so that when asked what would they like to see in the Social CRM initiative, superusers can brainstorm with an open mind. Using an external facilitator to manage the brainstorming session can ensure impartiality.

### Step 4: Needs-Analysis Questionnaires

The result of the brainstorming session is a list of non-prioritized business functional requirements that then need to be prioritized, along with validation of technical features and user-friendliness criteria noted during the brainstorming session. This is the reason for the needs-analysis questionnaire that is sent to a larger group of Social CRM system users. How many users? This is more a question of political correctness than one of statistical significance (between 50 and 100 users is typical). One global organization that I worked with sent the questionnaire to all its users so that everyone has some skin in the game. Three questionnaire types are typically sent to three decision-making groups: customer-facing personnel, managers, and executives. Although the three questionnaires may ask a few of the same questions, they should also ask specific questions that focus on the different decision-making responsibilities of each of the three groups. The questionnaires confirm and consolidate findings revealed during the field visits and the brainstorming session, as well as encourage the respondents to do a preliminary prioritization of the business functional needs and comment on identified technical features and user-friendliness criteria.

### Step 5: Business Process Review

Leverage the business process work that was completed during Step 6 in the Social CRM road map document (Chapter 8, "Getting Your Social CRM Strategy Right"). Create Visio diagrams or swim-lane charts for top business processes. "To-be" business processes should reflect best-in-class Social CRM business processes. This approach allows the organization to meet short-term Social CRM needs while planning for longer-term impact of Social Media communities and their growing impact on Social CRM.

### Step 6: Business Functional Prioritization

Identify prioritized business functions, based on the results of the field visits, the brainstorming session, the needs-analysis questionnaires, and the business process review. The results are presented to the Social CRM project team members.

### Step 7: Technical Platform Recommendations

Leverage the technical road map work completed in Step 5 in the Social CRM road map document. In view of the prioritized business functions and the technical baseline review results, make recommendations for appropriate technical platform enhancements for the Social CRM initiative, including software, hardware, and Social Media–to–Social CRM integration tools.

### Step 8: Social CRM Report

This report, which will be presented to the Social CRM project team for approval, should contain information needed to formulate the system specifications, including business and technical requirements.

### Step 9: Software Selection

If the decision is to use external software, consider looking at between three to five Social CRM software packages that are appropriate to the Social CRM business functions and technical features you have identified in Steps 1 through 8. Consider using an experienced, external Social CRM consultant to help write the request for proposal (RFP) and to review/select/negotiate with the organization's Social CRM vendor of choice.

### Step 10: Software Implementation Assistance

Software implementation is where the rubber meets the road. Some organizations use their own project manager and project implementation team. Other organizations use a Social CRM consultant to help implement the Social CRM project. The consultant

- selects the systems integrator, training partner, and recommended approach,
- evaluates project plans,
- participates in weekly operations review meetings,
- assists in implementing specific tasks/project management (for example, training manuals, pilot rules, and performance measurement criteria), and
- helps with other activities (for example, system assurance, customer satisfaction, and ongoing process improvements).

The Social CRM software selection process (Steps 1 through 10) typically takes eight to 12 weeks to complete (subtract two weeks for fast-track organizations and add four weeks for slow-track organizations). Regardless of the methodology used to select Social CRM software, be sure to use a structured approach similar to this ten-step methodology so that the *organization,* not the vendor, drives the process, and the organization ends up getting the software it really needs.

## Technical Requirements

The organization's Social CRM team must draft an initial list of technical-feature requirements during the Social CRM software selection process. These requirements should come directly from discussions with key stakeholders who helped develop the Social CRM system, as well as from IT personnel familiar with the organization's technology infrastructure.

Some confusion may arise between identifying the technical features of the Social CRM system, which facilitate the use of the software, and technical platform issues, which deal with the architecture required to support the Social CRM system. Decisions concerning technical platform issues most often rest with the IT department.

Here are some examples of technical platform issues:

- Will the Social CRM system have a net-native (hosted on the web), web-centric (browser-based) architecture, or is a web-enabled client/server architecture adequate?

- What operating system server environments will be compatible with the Social CRM system?

- What operating systems will be used in an organization's laptops, tablets, smartphones, and other devices? Does the software support responsive design, or are there separate apps for the mobile devices? How does the system synchronize data between the server, laptops, and mobile devices?

- How will the Social CRM system be accessed (Internet/web, virtual private networks, LAN and/or wireless technology)?

- What data integration tools are available in the Social CRM system for integrating social insight coming from Social Media community monitoring tools?

- How will data be synchronized between Social Media communities and the Social CRM system and users (servers, databases, and locations)?

- Will the organization's technical infrastructure and data storage capacity accommodate an on-premises Social CRM software solution, or does it make more sense to outsource the Social CRM software to a hosted or cloud solution?

- Will the organization's technical infrastructure integrate the current phone system into the Social CRM solution for use by contact center or help desk personnel?

- Which database(s) will the organization use for its Social CRM system (for example, IBM DB2, MS-SQL Server, Oracle, Sybase, and so on)? What will be the number and location of database servers required?

- Are the middleware (for example, Oracle's BEA, Scribe, Tibco, and so on) components in place to allow integration of back-office or legacy system data into the Social CRM solution? Do these solutions (or the ones built in-house) accommodate the bidirectional exchange of information?

- Should the organization move to more advanced data-sharing technologies, such as web services, XML, or SOAP-based technologies, to interconnect legacy systems with the Social CRM system?

- Should a data warehouse solution be integrated with the Social CRM solution? If yes, what tools are needed to derive the maximum value from the Social CRM solution: data transformation tools (for example, Informatica, Oracle Warehouse Builder, and SAP BusinessObjects Data Integrator) or data mining tools (for example, IBM-Cognos, SAAS, and SAP's KXEN/Business Objects/Crystal Reports)?

- What security features are available to protect the Social CRM system data?

- Will existing computer hardware support the Social CRM system? If not, what new hardware will be required?

Here are two tips about the technical features of a Social CRM system that impact software ease-of-use:

- Technical features are required in a Social CRM system to facilitate the implementation of the organization's prioritized business functional requirements. For example, if Social Media analytics is a prioritized business function, the organization will want to ensure that the software selected has the appropriate technical features to provide for comprehensive Social Media analytics. Alternatively, be sure the database is intuitive to system users if the Social CRM database is important for collaboration purposes.

- Learn about possible technical features by reviewing existing Social CRM software. Review some of the many packaged and hosted Social CRM software solutions to gain insight into the latest thinking about technical features.

An organization's IT department and/or an external consultant typically works with Social CRM users to determine what technical features should be included in the Social CRM software. Nevertheless, Social CRM users play an important role as reality checkers in evaluating technical features.

Technical features should not be judged on their wizardry, but on their business value. I worked on a Social CRM assignment with a publishing company in which the project leader had a technical background. During the system specification meeting, he showed me the latest technical features for Social CRM. Although many of the proposed technical features would be valuable to his company's Social CRM efforts, other features were little more than technical toys. To bring reality to the playing field, I asked the project leader about the top-five business functional requirements for the proposed system. After getting only two out of five correct, he began to listen more carefully to user needs.

Some of the greatest benefits that technical features can provide is their ability to help users feel comfortable with the system, to enable them to access and navigate the system, and to help make the system intuitive to their needs.

# Writing the Social CRM System Specifications

Upon completion of the Social CRM system needs analysis, prioritized business functional requirements, and technical features and user-friendliness/support requirements, the organization is ready now to write a Social CRM systems specifications document. This document forms the basis for the technical section of the RFP that is sent to a short list of qualified Social CRM vendors.

It is important to be sensitive to internal organizational rules and regulations regarding what is included in the RFP. The following are a few recommendations that can help structure a sound Social CRM system RFP:

- **General conditions section**—List general organizational conditions of significance, such as the right to reject, performance conditions, response verification, and conditions.

- **Vendor instructions**—Provide a clear description to the Social CRM vendor about the purpose of the specifications document, communications regarding the proposal, timetable for the proposal, selection and award process, vendor response deadlines, vendor presentation rules, and contract negotiations.

- **Proposal guidelines/formats**—Specify the format for the RFP response (typically done in electronic format), include a description of exceptions to the RFP, list what vendor contact information is required, and provide the RFP evaluation criteria (for example, the product features and operational capability consistent with specified requirements, the specialized relevant experience of the firm, completeness in addressing all aspects of the RFP, and the financial stability of the vendor).

- **Vendor profile**—Ask the vendor to provide the following types of background information:
  - Size of the company and whether it is local, national, or international
  - Location of the office that will handle your account
  - An affirmation that the vendor has a history of providing quality work
  - A profile of the vendor's product lines and industries served
  - A list of elements that differentiate the vendor from other organizations
  - The names of at least three clients that can be used as references

In addition to all the normal business functions and technical features that one expects to see in a CRM RFP, here is a short list of specific Social CRM criteria I ask the vendors to evaluate themselves against:

- Links/integration with public and private Social Media communities (for example, Facebook, Twitter, Pinterest, and so on), blogs, and online forums
- Social Media dashboard (for example, social channel aggregators)
- Activity feeds/microblogging
- Access to video spots
- Access to mashups
- Access to widget technologies
- Access to wiki databases
- Access to podcasts
- Access to tagging capabilities

- Social Media monitoring
- Social Media post routing
- Social Media information archive
- Social Media analytics

# Vendor RFP Response Review and Social CRM Demo

Once the vendors have submitted their RFP responses, the next step is to review their responses and to invite between one and three vendors to demonstrate their software at the organization's facilities. It usually takes an average of three to five hours per demonstration. Ask the vendors to demonstrate the functions and features they responded to positively in their RFP response document to keep them focused on the organization's specific needs.

To help ensure a realistic assessment of the software, ask the vendors to set up their software on organization equipment or to create a technical environment similar to the one that the organization is likely to use for the eventual system (for example, with 10,000-plus user records loaded onto the system).

If the organization's IT department will be building the Social CRM system, the system specifications document would, obviously, concentrate on business functional requirements, technical feature requirements, and user-support requirements, omitting information requests pertaining to the vendor's history.

Take time to carefully write a system-specifications document that will be sent to a qualified short list of external vendors in an RFP or by internal IT personnel. This will improve the chances that the Social CRM system you end up using closely mirrors the identified specifications.

## *Questions to Ask Social CRM Software Providers*

It is important to have a structured process for selecting the best Social CRM software vendor—they come and go, and technology enhancements often shake the very base on which vendors build their applications. Keep these potential difficulties in mind while asking each short-listed vendor the 12 questions that follow. But first, here are two cautions: If a short-listed vendor is evasive when responding to *any* of the questions, continue to request answers at that time rather than later. Also, do not rely on any single answer as the basis for the vendor selection decision. Instead, get the answers to all 12 questions, and then use business judgment to decide how well the vendor's responses apply to the organization's specific set of needs.

### Question 1: How long has the vendor been in business and what is its business history?

The Social CRM software vendor Infor (which began in 2002 and has gone through an IPO, as well as a number of organizational acquisitions and structural reorganizations over the years) has, like most vendors, weathered good and bad times in the CRM and Social CRM marketplace. Infor has proven to be a resilient CRM and Social CRM player, with products that consistently score high in independent user reviews such as ISM's *The Guide to Social and Mobile Customer Relationship Management*. Longevity is not necessarily an essential characteristic of a solid vendor, but nonetheless has value.

Dozens of outstanding Social CRM vendors—several of which are today's market leaders—have been in business between one and 12 years, have quality Social CRM software offerings, and are likely to continue to enhance their Social CRM offerings. Some Social CRM vendors are public companies or are backed by venture capital, whereas other vendors are new to the Social CRM industry—no hard-and-fast rules exist about their long-term viability. Therefore, although the number of years in business is important, that fact alone is not sufficient to determine whether the vendor is an appropriate fit for the organization.

### Question 2: Does the vendor have experience and customers in the organization's industry sector?

Experience in the organization's particular industry can be quite important. Software vendors that demonstrate their understanding of how the industry works, including building industry best practices within their software offering, typically are a real plus. Do not be swayed by a vendor's demonstration of industry-specific software because creating impressive demonstrations using today's software tools is reasonably easy. More important, ask questions about the vendor's active customers in the industry, and whether it is willing to provide the names of these customers along with contact information. Answers to these questions will help the organization to perform due diligence about how well a particular vendor has met the needs of other industry customers.

### Question 3: What is the vendor's technological direction (web strategy, Social CRM module-expansion intentions, and so on)?

It is important to understand the technology direction of each Social CRM vendor, and how well this direction fits the organization's technological direction. The best way to determine this is to hold a half-day technology session with the vendor's CTO. The objective of this session is to determine where the vendor is headed (for example, new business modules, new development tools, and the likely timeframes for each), to reveal what the organization's specific business functions and technical features are today and in the future, and to understand how well the vendor's offering meets these needs today and in the future. Be prepared to sign a nondisclosure agreement, which is standard for these types of meetings.

### Question 4: Who are the members of vendor's management team and what are their backgrounds?

The cumulative background and experience of a vendor's management team provides insight into the stability and credibility of the vendor. Look for a mix of business discipline backgrounds (for example, accounting, finance, information systems, operations, and others), as well as industry background (healthcare, consumer packaged goods, and so on). Also, look into the companies at which the vendor management team was previously employed. Are those companies thriving? Do they still exist?

### Question 5: How is the vendor financed?

Determine the financial backing of the Social CRM vendor. Is it a public company? Is it a private company? Is it a venture-capital backed company? Ownership can influence vendor behavior. For example, venture capital groups finance many new high-tech companies, particularly software companies. In many cases, the payback periods for the venture capital funds are very aggressive, so the venture capitalists want to be paid back in a short period of time. Therefore, the software vendor may feel additional pressure to sell as many seats or licenses as it can as quickly as possible. If the venture capital organization has dictated an exit strategy by acquisition, there is also increased pressure on the software vendor to do whatever it deems necessary to make the financials look attractive. Be sure to go beyond the financial statements when reviewing the financial stability of the vendor in question.

### Question 6: Is source code included with the product?

Increasingly, vendors are providing toolkits that let the customer make changes to the software without using third-party implementation partners. Much of the underlying code is programmed into reusable objects. Nevertheless, especially for on-premises software, not receiving software source code with the software purchase can limit an organization's ability to customize the Social CRM system without the help of vendor technicians or third-party implementation partners. If the vendor does not provide the source code, ask why not. What happens to the source code if the vendor goes out of business? Does the organization get the source code to ensure that the Social CRM system will continue to function? Pay close attention to the fine print regarding what is and what is not provided.

### Question 7: What training is offered for end users, the trainers, and systems administrators?

Remember that over the life of the Social CRM system, the cost of training will probably be up to five times the cost of the software. Does the vendor provide training? Is it provided in-house, on-site, or online? Does the vendor pass the training responsibility on to the resellers or implementation partners? Regardless of whether the vendor offers some or all needed training programs, ask how the vendor measures the performance of its own trainers, and how it measures the effectiveness of its training at the end-user reseller and end-user levels. Does the vendor have structured plans for ongoing training, refresher training, and training for new hires? Is the vendor using the latest technologies to provide training services, such as web-based training?

### Question 8: How does the vendor support its software (does it have a guaranteed response time)?

Many vendors provide support services as part of their maintenance agreement. Find out what types of support are offered as part of the maintenance agreement (for example, phone support, web-based self-service, and/or on-site). Some offer a la carte support programs such as pay-per-incident and per-support interaction. Are the support services passed on from the vendor to the third-party implementation partner? If the vendor's support services are "outsourced" to a third-party company, what certification programs does the vendor have to teach, train, and certify third-party partner personnel?

### Question 9: What is included in the maintenance agreement (what is the fixed number of upgrades per year)?

Maintenance programs provided by Social CRM vendors can vary greatly in cost and complexity. Get specifics on exactly what is provided by the agreement, the timeframe of the agreement, and who will provide the service and support (the vendor and/or the vendor's implementation/ service partner). Ask the vendor how upgrades and updates will be made available—whether via a download from a website or via a reseller. Will the organization have access to a dedicated technician or group of technicians by phone, email, or website? Does the vendor guarantee a specific turnaround time for problem resolution? What kind of resources has the vendor devoted to its support/service options?

### Question 10: What is the warranty period and bug-fix policy during this period?

Find out what type of warranty policy a vendor has for its products. Many vendors offer a standard 90-day warranty period, but ask the vendor what is included in this warranty. Find out from the vendor how, when, and where software fixes, updates, and upgrades are made available. Also ask the vendor about the extension of the warranty and any costs associated with these extensions.

### Question 11: How does the vendor implement the software (by itself or via a third-party implementer)?

Most Social CRM vendors provide comprehensive product suites that employ the services of third-party implementation partners. If the vendor provides the implementation using its own technical staff, how many consultants are dedicated to implementation efforts? Does the vendor provide any type of rapid-implementation option? If so, is it appropriate to the organization's business situation? Ask questions about the qualifications of the vendor's implementation staff. In the case of third-party implementation partners, find out about the type of certification and length of training required to become a vendor-implementation partner. In the event that the vendor uses third-party implementation partners, ask how the vendor ensures the quality of these partners. Make sure that the vendor and/or the implementation partners are actually using the Social CRM software for their own Social CRM operations.

### Question 12: How important is your business to the vendor?

Will the organization be an important customer to the vendor? Will the vendor commit the necessary resources to ensure the successful implementation of the organization's Social CRM system? To make sure the software vendor provides appropriate attention, some customers insist that they be members of the software vendor's "board of advisors" or equivalent. Regardless how it gets done, secure guarantees from the software vendor that it is prepared to commit the necessary resources to make the organization's Social CRM project a success.

Once you have the answers to these 12 questions, apply business judgment to determine which of these questions are most applicable to the success of the project. Then decide which software vendor best meets the organization's needs. A recommendation: When sizing up a Social CRM software vendor, determine the fit between the organization's Social CRM project direction and that of the vendor. Think of it as a marriage—the organization and the vendor are entering into a long-term relationship. Ask the hard questions early on.

## Tips for Negotiating with Social CRM Vendors

Gartner states that Social CRM vendors took more than 40 percent of the market share for campaign management at the beginning of 2014. Gartner goes on to say that by the end of 2015, digital strategies such as social marketing will influence at least 80 percent of consumers' discretionary spending, thus leading new entrants into the growing Social CRM marketplace.[1]

This is good news for Social CRM software buyers—it strengthens the organization's position in a negotiation. Many excellent Social CRM software vendors need the business now, and are willing to negotiate substantial discounts regardless of what the official company policies suggest.

I regularly help ISM customers negotiate with vendors, and although I am respectful of them, I also am very aware of vendor margins and what can and cannot be negotiated. I helped a payroll services company client to secure a 52 percent discount on the list price from a mid-market leader. In the end, ISM secured a 500-person license deal, inclusive of implementation services, for a cost of $682,000 ($1,364 per seat), down from the initial bid of $1.4 million.

The following negotiating tips work well in a buyers' market. Organizations are well advised either to do their homework up front to determine the competitive Social CRM software pricing or to engage an external advisor who knows market pricing.

- Be sure to understand the need for each optional software module being recommended by the vendor. ("What is the value-add for each of the recommended optional software modules?") Be particularly sensitive to the vendor's desire to scale up its perception of any part of the organization's business (especially if the vendor happens to excel in this area).

- Include as many of the vendor's optional modules as possible into the base agreement. Lock in pricing in the initial negotiation regardless of when the modules will actually be put to use.

- Ensure that the agreement is as definitive as possible. All vendors are prepared to negotiate adding new clauses, modifying existing clauses, and even deleting clauses in their standard agreement.

- Spread payment for the software over the life of the agreement. Although most vendors do not like to spread out payments, more vendors are prepared to do this to secure business.

- If the vendor is also providing implementation services, list and define the deliverables and/or acceptance criteria within the agreement, and be sure that they have clearly defined metrics. Peg payments to the successful achievement of deliverables/acceptance criteria. Here is one possible payment model: 20 percent of payment upon signing the agreement, 20 percent on the successful accomplishment of an initial set of deliverables/acceptance criteria, an additional 20 percent on the successful accomplishment of the next set of deliverables/acceptance criteria, and the final 40 percent upon the successful accomplishment of a final set of deliverable/acceptance criteria.

- When using the vendor or one of its partners for implementation services, purchase a block of the vendor's program and project managers' time or of the Social CRM vendor implementation consultants' time to secure a discount rate.

- Consider requesting a site license for your organization on a national and/or international basis. When considering site-license pricing, determine the current expected number of Social CRM users (let's call this variable "x"), as well as the expected number of Social CRM users within 12 to 24 months (let's call this variable "y"). Negotiate the site license based on a price that is as close to "y" as is possible.

- Maintenance charges certainly can and should be negotiated. Calculate the annual maintenance charge with the percent discount coming off of the net price (what you actually pay) rather than on the list price. The asking price for maintenance may be 18 to 22 percent, but you should negotiate a percentage between 12 and 18 percent. Start the maintenance charges after the system has received final acceptance; it is not unreasonable to have the maintenance charges begin up to 12 months after final acceptance of the system. Alternatively, negotiate one free year of maintenance, either from the date that the agreement is signed or the date the system was accepted.

- Do not purchase all licenses up front. Structure the agreement so that the organization initially purchases little more than a developer server license and a limited number of user licenses to be deployed during the Social CRM pilot. The vendor may not like this approach. Although it might cost the organization a bit more, this approach has worked well for many of my clients.

- Negotiate with the vendor at the close of its quarter. Even better, negotiate with the vendor at the close of its fiscal year, when discounts will be at their highest rate.

The current buyers' market will not last forever, but it's quite likely that Social CRM software vendors will continue to welcome new business. Limits exist to vendor discounts, along with the need to ensure a good spirit of partnership when the negotiations have been completed, but there is plenty of negotiating room when cutting a fair deal with Social CRM vendors.

I often ask, "If one can run a multimillion-dollar equity portfolio on Quicken's software that costs less than $100 to purchase, why does the per-user cost for Social CRM software run between $300 and $1,200 per year for Cloud software and why is one-time price for on-premises software between $800 and $2,000?"

Social CRM software vendors will appropriately suggest the per-user cost of their software needs to be weighed against the value that their software delivers, but I'm convinced that Social CRM software prices will continue to come down.

In the next chapter, I dig into the ten steps that an organization needs to take to realize a successful Social CRM implementation.

# Endnotes

1. Gartner, "Digital Marketing: The Critical Trek for Multichannel Campaign Management," http://www.gartner.com/newsroom/id/1607814 (March 2011).

# 10

## Ten Steps to Effective Social CRM Implementation

Social CRM remains a mystery to many corporate executives despite its many benefits. Why? Mainly because the technological issues associated with automating Social CRM tasks intimidate them and because they have not had an opportunity to review a structured approach for successfully implementing Social CRM. That's why I have developed a ten-step approach to help organizations implement Social CRM successfully.

My experience suggests that when executives follow the ten steps outlined in this chapter, they greatly improve the likelihood that their organization's Social CRM implementation will succeed. My experience also indicates that missing any of these steps greatly increases the likelihood that the Social CRM implementation will be bogged down, will fail, or will become a dinosaur soon after implementation.

### Step 1: Organize the Project Management Team

Initially, a project team should comprise the following:

- **A project champion**, preferably a senior executive, who will be responsible for ensuring appropriate managerial and financial backing throughout the project. The project champion will be involved about an average of six hours per month during the 6- to 12-month project lifecycle.

- **A project manager** who has business process and technical skills. This person will be responsible for implementing the project day to day. This will usually be a full-time position during the project's lifecycle.

- **A project user group** comprising Social CRM end users who are responsible for providing input to the project leader during the project's conceptualization phase, and who test the system during the design and implementation phases. The group will be involved about an average of eight hours per month during the 6- to 12-month project lifecycle.

## Step 2: Determine the Functions to Automate

Effective Social CRM at an organization starts with selecting the Social CRM software (see the ten-step methodology described in Chapter 9, "Social CRM Software Selection and Vendor Negotiation"). This process identifies the business functions that need to be automated and lists the technical features that are required in the Social CRM system. Although several different software-selection-process methodologies are available, I favor one that contains questionnaires, face-to-face interviews with customer-facing personnel, face-to-face interviews with customers (if possible), visits with sales representatives in the field and/or customer service reps in the contact center, as well as sales channel partners, a review of existing and planned business processes, a technical assessment, and a final report.

Some organizations opt to hire an external Social CRM consultant to guide the process; others prefer to implement the process themselves. If the latter is chosen, start by assigning the task of selecting the Social CRM software to a project team comprising internal and/or external personnel familiar with the organization's sales, marketing, and customer service operations. It may be a good idea to send one or more members of the project team to a Social CRM seminar in which implementation details are discussed (for example, the annual CRM Evolution event or the annual Gartner Customer Summit event).

Regardless of the approach, the Social CRM software selection process is a critical deliverable. If it is not performed properly, it is likely that the organization will not be in a position to implement an effective Social CRM system. In my experience, organizations that take the time to select their software properly have more easily and quickly realized the benefits of Social CRM than those organizations that did not. The latter are now paying the price in wasted time, effort, and money.

Remember to automate only that which needs automating. For example, automating an inefficient business process can be a costly mistake.

During a visit with the CIO of a leading Italian fashion house, he told me he wanted to use the Social CRM system to "once and for all control [the] unstructured Italian sales force's sales and marketing processes." To approach and use Social CRM to try to control a sales force's unstructured sales and marketing processes is a grave error. Consequently, this company's Social CRM system never took off.

To ensure that the organization automates that which needs to be automated, the Social CRM software selection process should address a wish list of how salespeople, marketing personnel, customer support employees, executives, and customers would like to improve their work processes. The top salesman at one organization expressed to me the following wish during the Social CRM software selection process:

> "If only I could get updated information on both my potential client and my competitors prior to the sales call."

Remember that the people doing the job know how to do it better. By taking time to work with them, the organization will learn what needs to be automated.

## Step 3: Gain Top Executive Support/ Commitment

Organizations that successfully automate the customer-facing functions view Social CRM systems as business tools rather than technological tools. Keep this in mind as top executives are approached for support.

Top executive commitment can be secured by demonstrating that Social CRM

- supports the business strategy (because Social CRM delivers information required to make key decisions that enable a business strategy to be realized),
- measurably impacts and improves results,
- significantly reduces costs (and thus pays for itself over a specified time period), and
- documents the case for Social CRM based on business impact.

## Step 4: Employ Technology Smartly

Select Social CRM information technology and systems that use open architecture. It makes it easy to enhance and enlarge the system over time. Look for software applications that are modularized and can be easily integrated into or interconnected with the organization's existing information databases. Ensure the technology selected is portable. For firms conducting business between the field and headquarters or across regions, select software applications that are network compatible and that permit easy web connection and/or data synchronization between information on field computers, tablets, and mobile devices and on regional or headquarter computers. To accommodate future changes, be sure the selected technology can easily be customized and modified. In other words, let the technology help the organization grow.

Although technology is only one step in the overall approach for successfully implementing Social CRM, it is vital to the functioning of Social CRM systems. Users should be familiar with leading technologies that will continue to help drive customer acceptance of Social CRM in the future. A detailed discussion of these leading technologies can be found in Chapter 18, "Social CRM Technology Issues."

## Step 5: Secure User Ownership

Get users involved early to make sure that the Social CRM system addresses their needs. One large information technology manufacturer automated its Social Media efforts in accordance with the results of the corporate headquarters' Social CRM task force. The actual end users were not sufficiently represented on this task force and ended up revolting against what they felt was yet another "big brother" system.

Generally, Social CRM users will respond favorable to Social CRM when what I call the "3X factor" is in place. I define the 3X factor as follows: For every one piece of information that the user requests, the Social CRM system must provide at least three pieces of valuable information back to the user. When the 3X factor is in place, it motivates users to fully exploit the Social CRM system.

Remember that a satisfied user will want to work with the system, and no one knows better what users need and what they find annoying than the users themselves. Do not be afraid to hand over ownership of the system to the users.

## Step 6: Prototype the System

Prototyping the Social CRM system allows the organization to phase in new technology; experiment on a smaller and less costly scale; test the system's functionality; highlight required changes in organizational procedures; and, most important, demonstrate that Social CRM objectives can be met. The availability of rapid prototyping software development tools reinforces the importance of "testing before you leap."

## Step 7: Train Users

Training is a multistep process that should

- provide a demonstration to users on how to access and use information, including social insight information,
- ensure that users are provided with business process and Social CRM system documentation that is understandable and frequently updated,
- offer online tutorials that can be customized for each user,
- provide a phone help line to support the users, and
- train the trainers to ensure that new system users can be up and running quickly.

In many cases, using web-based training will help increase training effectiveness while reducing cost.

At a leading air courier express company, several members of the sales force requested that all information on the Social CRM system be printed on paper. This request stemmed from the fact that these users had not been properly trained and did not know how to properly navigate the system to obtain the needed information.

Over the life of the Social CRM system, training will end up costing between one and one-and-a-half times the cost of the Social CRM system hardware/software. Budget for training accordingly, and remember that the best way to change work habits and to ensure the system's success is via effective training.

## Step 8: Motivate Personnel

Social CRM succeeds when users are motivated by the system's ability to help them obtain their objectives. When users understand the strategic importance of Social CRM, there will be improved user productivity and a positive impact on the organization's bottom line.

Trends come and go within an organization, so determine ways to maintain individual motivation and commitment toward the Social CRM system. Show users their importance and their impact in the Social CRM system.

## Step 9: Administrate the System

One person or department must be held responsible for overseeing the welfare of the Social CRM system. This person or department must include an information gatekeeper, responsible for ensuring that all information is timely, relevant, easy to access, and positively impacts the users' decision-making needs. With Social CRM, securing usable social insight can be challenging.

It is one thing to have to be out in the field and using the Social CRM system with good data; it is another to find out-of-date or incorrect data. Be disciplined and pay careful attention to information and systems details.

## Step 10: Keep Management Committed

Set up a committee that includes senior employees and users from the sales, marketing, and customer service departments, as well as from the information systems department. This committee should brief senior executives quarterly concerning the status of the Social CRM system project, including successes, failures, future needs, growth, and other metrics. Measure the system's results and relay the impact of the system to management. Also, be sure to secure the "system's champion."

Social CRM's benefits can be enormous. They include the creation of two-way dialogues with customers and prospects as well as better engagement with them to drive sales, satisfaction, advocacy, and more.

To realize these benefits, however, the organization must set up a process to properly select the Social CRM software, take the ten steps described in this chapter, and address both technical and nontechnical Social CRM issues.

Chapter 11, "Social CRM: Achieving the Right Mix of People, Process, and Technology," examines the importance of obtaining the right mix of people, process, and technology for a Social CRM initiative.

# 11

## Social CRM: Achieving the Right Mix of People, Process, and Technology

In this chapter, I discuss the critical mix of three crucial components: the people, process, and technology that create healthy, two-way dialogues with customers. This critical mix must be adjusted throughout the initiative to ensure that Social CRM goals are met. Each of the components presents its own set of challenges that I examine in Part IV, "Social CRM—Process Issues." This chapter takes a more holistic approach, digging into why getting this mix right throughout the initiative is so important.

### The People, Process, and Technology Components

The *people* component presents the greatest challenge, because users are sensitive about change. Social CRM systems support and automate customer processes, and almost always require changes in the way users do their jobs day to day. Users who do not understand the point of these changes, who are not allowed to participate in their formulation, or who are not given adequate preparation and training will, understandably, resist the changes. Gaining user support early on is an important factor in the success of any Social CRM initiative, so be sure to address people issues from the outset.

The *process* component of Social CRM is the most delicate, because inappropriate use of automation will only quicken errant processes. Many organizations have well-established customer facing business processes (that is, those processes that directly interface with the customer during the purchase, payment, and use of the organization's products and services), but Social CRM will almost certainly require enhancements to existing customer-facing processes. Also, organizations pursuing a Social CRM initiative often try to correct customer-facing process deficiencies by purchasing Social CRM software that contains one or more business processes prebuilt by the Social CRM vendor and then forcing the not-built-here processes on system users. This can be dangerous. Process change should be driven from within.

The *technology* component of a Social CRM initiative is too often given a disproportionate emphasis, sometimes to the detriment of the overall project. A hyper-focus on technology is somewhat understand-able, considering the growing number of emerging technology solutions. In Social CRM initiatives, there are two primary concerns: the need to deal with software vendors and the challenge of staying on top of trends. On the upside, the Internet is an extremely useful technological tool for achieving important Social CRM goals.

Because the people, process, and technology mix changes through-out the initiative, ensuring that the mix is right through all phases of any implementation becomes critical its success.

Table 11.1 provides a generic model for understanding how the mix alters throughout key Social CRM implementation activities.

**Table 11.1**  Critical Social CRM Implementation Activities Mix

| Key Social CRM Implementation Activities | Most Relevant Components |
| --- | --- |
| Determining business requirements | People, some process |
| Setting up the project management team | People, some process |
| Integrating social insight from Social Media communities and other technical integrations | Technology |
| Customizing the Social CRM software | People, process, technology |
| Social CRM system pilot | People, technology |
| Social CRM system rollout | People, technology |
| Social CRM system support | People, some process |
| Growing the Social CRM system | People, process, technology |

Let's look at a few of the Social CRM implementation activities in Table 11.1 to better understand the dynamics of getting the mix right. First, a structured process must be applied to ensure that user needs are properly identified and prioritized to determine Social CRM business requirements. Most of the work in determining business requirements, however, involves people issues (working with potential users to think through their existing and future needs, and to help manage their expectations about how the initiative is likely to impact those needs). Technology plays a minor role, at best, in determining business requirements.

Similarly, the people component plays a critical role during the assembly of a Social CRM project management team. It's important to assign employees specific responsibilities for each implementation activity. There is also a need for process when determining how to optimally set up the project management team and subteams. Again, technology will have a limited role in this situation.

Technology becomes critical when the organization is ready to begin integrating Social Media information and other needed systems. Agreement on the appropriate technology platform and middleware toolset's use will impact the effectiveness and efficiency of required systems integration. People may insist that their system needs to be integrated first (and there should be a process for determining which systems to integrate and in which order), but, overall, technology drives this activity.

All three components play critical roles during Social CRM software customization. People are critical for judging how well the customizations meet their needs, as well as for commenting on how the workflow impacts the system's overall user friendliness. Process is important for driving workflow development (which, in turn, is built by technology). Technology is critical for developing, modifying, and deleting fields on an application's screen view and for navigating between screens. Clearly, all three components have their place—it's all about getting the mix right.

## Keeping Social CRM on a Healthy Track

Getting the people/process/technology mix right is finally beginning to take hold. I hear more and more Social CRM vendors and organizations talk about first getting the process component right, then addressing the change management (people) component early on, and, lastly, locking down the technology component.

Most organizations that purchase and apply Social CRM understand that an effective mix of people (50 percent), process (30 percent), and technology (20 percent) is the key driver of successful Social CRM implementations. These organizations are achieving success by putting customer-facing processes in order, then enticing personnel (internal, partners, customers, and so on) to buy into the enhanced processes, and then applying Social CRM technology in support of these enhanced pro-cesses. By following a proven Social CRM strategy and implementation methodology based on getting the people/process/technology mix right, many organizations are steering their way to Social CRM success.

Each of the next three parts of *The Definitive Guide to Social CRM* delve deeper into people, process, and technology issues, respectively. I also share more stories and describe additional best practices.

# Part IV
## Social CRM—Process Issues

# 12

## Realizing Effective Process Change

The process component of Social CRM is the most delicate because automating a broken Social CRM business process will only make this process worse—and do it quicker. A broken process will also negatively impact the success of the Social CRM implementation. Most organizations embarking on a Social CRM initiative typically have some Social Media business processes in place (that is, processes that directly interface with internal/external Social Media communities), but these processes often need enhancement.

### Key Business—Process Success Criteria

The first step is to assess the current Social CRM processes. What is working, what is not, and where are enhancements required? It is not wrong to look at the built-in processes housed in a Social CRM software package, but Social CRM is more successful when new or enhanced processes are driven internally. They will better reflect the exact needs and culture of the organization.

These seven business-process success criteria help to ensure a structured approach:

- **Ownership**—Does each Social CRM process have an owner? If no one owns the process, it tends not to get implemented with excellence, and if more than one person owns a process, there tends to be chaos.
- **Goals**—Does each process have clear goals?
- **Metrics**—Are performance standards and metrics routinely used to determine the processes' success from both a company and customer viewpoint? Are these metrics regularly being measured?

- **Interfaces**—Are there any internal or external process or system interfaces that the Social CRM process is integrated with where customer information flows? Are the interfaces in place and do they work well?

- **Documentation**—Have the key steps within the process been documented and agreed on by process owners and customer-facing users? Have users ever seen this documentation? Is it a part of their training curriculum?

- **Integrity**—Is the Social CRM process being implemented by all users in the same way, regardless of who implements it and where?

- **Fit with business vision**—Do the Social CRM processes directly support the organization's business vision? The tighter this support, the stronger the support for the process.

Once relevant Social CRM processes have been assessed, create a matrix showing how each process scores against these success criteria. Then prioritize the identified Social CRM processes based on business impact, and determine the best way to enhance each prioritized process.

## Social CRM Process Business Case Examples

Here are four examples that underscore the importance of implementing new or enhanced Social CRM processes in a structured manner.

### A Global Manufacturer

This global B2C manufacturer created a private Social Media community as a part of its digital strategy. The community was seen as an important way to open a two-way dialogue with end customers, and to secure input from these customers for use in both the organization's Social CRM efforts and product development efforts (ideation). Securing meaningful content to ensure there was something to talk about during the initial weeks/months of the community was one of the core business processes at the outset. The community content process that identified internal and external content providers (for example, bloggers and consumer data sheet specialists) was put into place, setting up the community content calendar as well as describing what was due by whom and when. The organization created several other Social CRM processes (for example, the membership process and the monitoring process) and implemented them en route to a very successful private Social Media community. The structured approach was applied for each process.

## A Consumer Goods Manufacturer

This global consumer goods organization embarked on a Social CRM initiative that included the creation and automation of the key account management process. Unfortunately, the organization encountered problems from the start. Rather than using internal inputs to map the process, which was to have included monitoring and filtering information about key accounts from public Social Media websites, the organization decided to look for a Social CRM software vendor that incorporated the key account management process into its software. The organization located a vendor that offered a generic key account management process in its software application that it said could easily import social insight coming from Social Media communities. The organization purchased the software and trained its personnel on how to use the software's key account management process.

During the software training, users became increasingly uncomfortable with the capabilities of the software's key account management process. Users-in-training thought the process did not easily capture social insight about key accounts from public Social Media communities. Monitoring and filtering capabilities were cumbersome, and importing captured social insight into the key account management functionality that sat within the internal Social CRM system was complicated.

After much debate, the organization decided to place the Social CRM initiative on hold until it had specified its Social Media filtering and integration process internally, which it did with the full backing of potential process users. Next, the organization trained all key account management personnel on the new process to secure their feedback and eventual buy-in for the enhanced process. Last, it issued an RFP to a handful of Social CRM vendors based on the internally generated key account management process specification.

The organization discovered that the following steps would help it maximize the effectiveness of the Social CRM initiative:

- Rely first on internally generated processes (preferably with employee participation).

- Document and train on new or modified processes.
- Look into Social CRM software tools to help make the Social CRM processes work more efficiently.

## A Global Life Sciences Organization

This global life sciences organization decided to revamp its lead management business process before upgrading its Social CRM software. Why? Prior to the process upgrade, sales leads came from a variety of Social Media sources, including the company's Social Media communities on Facebook, LinkedIn, and Twitter, online communities, blogs, and so on. The organization's marketing department quickly screened all leads before they were assigned to field sales personnel based on region and/or area of specialization. However, two kinks emerged in this approach:

- First, the marketing department did not have sufficient time to qualify leads during busy periods.
- Second, the marketing department was hesitant to send out unqualified Social Media leads to field sales personnel.

As a result, leads often remained in the marketing department until they could be qualified, which translated into delays of days or weeks during which time the lead often went cold. When the marketing department did send leads to field sales personnel, it often sent them in batches with little or no prioritized ranking of the leads. Too often, the busy field sales personnel simply did not follow up on these leads.

The company gathered sales, marketing, and the top executives together to create an ideal lead-management process to correct the situation. Social Media comments/information were designated as A (ultra-hot), B (hot), C (warm), and D (cold). Designations were made based on a number of agreed-upon, weighted criteria (for example, contact method, product interest, and type of application). The new, internally driven lead-management process was accepted and promoted effectively throughout the company. Next, all marketing and sales personnel received training on the new process. Last, the new process was automated using Social CRM software workflow tools.

Now the new lead-management process takes leads from Social Media sites and, using a workflow, proceeds to filter each lead by passing it through a popular online lead-qualification engine and then sends the lead directly to the appropriate field sales reps (with a copy to marketing personnel) for follow-up.

### Another Global Manufacturer

Another global manufacturing company (a B2B organization) proposed to modify its sales pipeline process that also started with securing leads off Social Media sites. By mapping this process, the manufacturer determined its sales pipeline process currently had seven steps, and a sales opportunity took on average six months to close. The vice president of sales thought that a tighter sales pipeline process supported by Social CRM tools would help decrease the amount of time it took to close an opportunity by one month (from six to five months).

During this period, however, the company also learned that delays in the sales pipeline process were not necessarily the result of sales department delays. Instead, they were often a result of inefficiencies in other departmental processes that impacted the sales pipeline process. For example, sales personnel depended on the corporate and legal departments to approve key documents, which were routinely late, to complete the third step of the process. In other words, decreasing the sales process from six to five months depended as much on streamlining how the sales pipeline process integrated with other departments involved in the process as it did on helping sales personnel to efficiently sell more.

A critical step in the final, enhanced sales-pipeline process allowed sales personnel to engage with leads and customers in their channel of choice, including the new Social Media channel from where many of this organization's leads were being generated.

## Social CRM Process Business Case Takeaways

It should be clear from these four examples that Social CRM software is neither the issue nor the answer to realizing effective process change. It cannot mend a broken process. People mend or enhance business processes by following a structured approach that starts with an assessment of a current state of key sales, marketing, and customer service processes. They then enhance these processes based on valuable, internally driven input, along with external best practices. Then and only then can Social CRM software be brought in to drive efficiency into these now sound business processes.

I dig deeper into the structure of a business process review in Chapter 13, "Understanding Business Process Review," because sound business processes remain critical for the success or failure of a Social CRM initiative.

# 13

## Understanding Business Process Review

The success of any organization's Social CRM initiative depends on the quality of existing and future business processes that lead to the marketing, purchase, payment, and use of the organization's products and services. Social CRM provides the opportunity to enhance existing processes and create new ones that leverage Social Media's explosive growth.

## Ten-Step Business Process Review

The following ten-step business process review methodology provides general guidelines for the activities that must take place to achieve Social CRM business-process excellence.

### Step 1: Meet with the Business Process Participants to Plan an Initial Schedule

Meet with the key business process review leaders to determine a strategy, direction, and list of possible participants in the business process review. Participants typically include customer-facing personnel (who work day to day with customers) and process SMEs (the personnel who typically own the key business processes). Outline a tentative timeline for completing the ten-step review for all participants.

### Step 2: Research Relevant Social CRM Industry Best Practices

Review relevant Social CRM industry best practices in view of what is learned in Step 1 and, where feasible, include process-flow documents for each best practice.

## Step 3: Interview Customer Personnel about Current State of Business Processes

Set up interviews/meetings with process SMEs to determine Social CRM processes as they are in sales, marketing, and customer service. Assess each business processes on the following seven criteria, which were introduced in Chapter 8, "Getting Your Social CRM Strategy Right," and are expanded on in Chapter 12, "Realizing Effective Process Change."

- **Ownership**—Is there clear responsibility, authority, and accountability for the success of the process? Does each Social CRM process have an owner? If more than one person owns a process, there tends to be chaos. If no one owns the process, it tends not to get implemented with excellence.

- **Goals**—Does each process have clear goals?

- **Metrics**—Are performance standards and metrics routinely used to determine the process's success from both a company and customer viewpoint? Are these metrics being measured on a regular basis?

- **Interfaces**—Are there any internal or external process or system interfaces that the Social CRM process is integrated with where customer information flows? Are the interfaces in place and do they work well?

- **Documentation**—Have the key steps within the process been documented and agreed on by process owners and customer-facing users? Have users ever seen this documentation? Is it a part of their training curriculum?

- **Integrity**—Is the Social CRM process being implemented by all users in the same way regardless of who implements it and where?

- **Fit with business vision**—Does the Social CRM process directly support the organization's business vision? The tighter this support, the stronger the support for the process.

During these interviews, note any potential quick wins or other ideas that could impact the draft to-be process flows in preparation for Step 8.

## Step 4: Document As-Are Processes and Make Best-in-Class Comparisons

Based on the data collected in Step 3, map the Social CRM as-are process flows (there are several good ways to perform this mapping with "fish-line" tools, which is one of the more effective methods). If best in class has been determined, compare as-are process flows to industry benchmarks.

## Step 5: Collect Feedback on As-Are Process Flows

Send process flows and documentation to process SMEs with a list of ideas that may have been culled from the research conducted in Step 2. Request that customer personnel review the process flows and documentation, and provide feedback regarding needed enhancements. Make updates to process flows and documentation based on this feedback.

## Step 6: Hold Workshop(s) to Review Feedback

Meet with customer-facing personnel to discuss any "ah-ha" insights gathered from the review of as-are business processes. Collect and discuss missing process steps or clarifications of documented steps. Document participant feedback.

## Step 7: Hold a Business Process Improvement Workshop

Set up a workshop (lasting two-and-a-half to four hours) to review as-are process flows and to develop preliminary to-be process flows. Workshop participants should include both customer-facing personnel and process SMEs. Outcomes from this workshop typically include the following:

- Preliminary to-be process flows
- Goals and objectives for these to-be processes
- To-be process assumptions
- Proposed to-be process metrics
- Other to-be process issues and considerations
- Activities and efforts to be involved in flushing out the to-be process work

### Step 8: Draft To-Be Process Flows

Process SMEs develop Level 1 and Level 2 to-be process flows based on the output of the workshop in Step 7. Level 1 represents the highest level of the process steps and notes additional processes that are culled from the key process. Level 2 process flows provide process details for each key activity/step in the Level 1 process flow. Leverage best-in-class Social CRM practices throughout the development of to-be processes. To-be process flows should include documentation of high-level activities, decisions, and flow of information, including the process interfaces with other business functions, individuals, and systems.

### Step 9: Hold a Business Process To-Be Workshop

Set up a workshop to review and enhance to-be process flows. Workshop participants again typically include both customer-facing personnel and process SMEs. This workshop typically lasts two-and-a-half to four hours and provides time to vet, change, or modify ideas and suggestions that may enhance to-be processes. The workshop output is an agreed-on set of to-be process flows and a list of key actions needed to complete documentation of these flows.

### Step 10: Finalize Process Recommendations

Present to-be processes back to customer-facing personnel and process SMEs for final approval. Next, prioritize to-be processes that will be incorporated into the Social CRM initiative based on the following criteria:

- Urgency (what is needed for Phase 1 of Social CRM implementation)
- Potential impact (customer intimacy, revenue enhancement, cost reduction, efficiency improvement, and others)
- Available resources (personnel identified to implement to-be processes)
- An action plan (to operationalize prioritized to-be processes)

To summarize, the ten-step business process review

- develops an understanding of Social CRM needs from the perspective of customer-facing personnel and customers,

- creates a visual model of existing or as-is business processes that impact these Social CRM needs,
- identifies gaps in process requirements, and
- enhances existing processes or creates new to-be processes in support of Social CRM needs.

Finally, here's one additional point regarding the role of customers in this ten-step business process review: I am all in favor of inviting customers to participate throughout the process review. They are in a unique position to provide meaningful feedback regarding customer-facing processes that will impact how they do business with the organization. However, I am also aware that not all organizations are willing to involve customers in what the organization may consider to be internal activities. My advice: Get customers involved in the process wherever possible based on the organization's comfort level.

## Business Process Improvements Must Precede Technology Implementation

A crucial element in the success of a Social CRM implementation is that business process improvements precede technology implementation. On a recent vacation in Milano Marittima, a small town on the Adriatic Sea, I had the pleasure of watching Germany win a major soccer tournament against Argentina. I was impressed by how well the German team played, but more important I was struck by how structured its playbook was. The team had many plays and had practiced them time and time again, until they had become second nature. If only organizations implemented Social CRM in a similar manner.

The right way to implement a Social CRM initiative is to first determine what Social CRM business functions management wants its initiative to address (for example, sales, marketing, customer service, and so on) and how these functions will integrate social insight from Social Media community monitoring and filtering. Taking into account the new to-be processes, prioritize these business functions (remembering to bite off only what the organization is able to chew), since successful Social CRM initiatives get rolled out in multiple iterations. Take the time to train customer-facing personnel and customers on how to use the new processes. Last, apply Social CRM technology to optimize the organization's well-thought-out Social CRM business processes.

Unfortunately, too many organizations depend on Social CRM software vendors to supply needed Social CRM business processes. This is backward logic: Increasingly, software vendors build valuable Social CRM process capabilities directly into their software (for example, Social CRM software vendor Salesforce.com does a nice job integrating its Radian6 monitoring platform into its Social CRM platform, whereas Social Media platform vendor Mzinga builds in Social Media listening, moderation, and social analytics capabilities directly into its software). However, many Social CRM software vendors are not sufficiently business-process savvy to know which specific Social CRM processes to offer in their software. Therefore, they default to offering one of two options:

- Building in generic processes along with a business process/ workflow engine. This helps to customize the generic processes to varying degrees, which may or may not fit the organization's way of doing business.

- Offering vertical, industry-specific software that builds in relevant, industry-specific business processes to varying degrees that, again, may or may not fit well with what management needs.

Unfortunately, neither of these two options is optimal.

A third option, practiced by best-in-class organizations worldwide, is to follow the ten-step business process review. It delivers valuable, prioritized Social CRM business processes that drive Social CRM success. It allows the organization to select a Social CRM software vendor that can actually deliver that organization's Social CRM business process needs.

In the event that no vendor can deliver exactly what is required, be sure to review the business process/workflow engine that each vendor offers with its software to determine whether this engine, together with a bit of ingenuity and elbow grease, can deliver what the organization is requesting.

That brings me back to the topic of Germany's soccer tournament victory. Knowing the plays was a part of the German team's DNA. The team then executed these plays with excellence. Think of the processes in an organization as the plays and the Social CRM software as the players. Get the plays right, then choose and train the best players.

In the next chapter, I focus specifically on applying business-process best practices to create the Social Media component of a successful Social CRM initiative.

# 14

## Applying "Process" Best Practices to Social Media Strategy

I use a three-stage process (contemplate, navigate, and calibrate) to design a successful Social Media strategy that will deliver successful Social Media communities. As noted in Chapter 4, "Leverage Social Media Information to Advance Your Social CRM Efforts" (where I described the Social CRM framework), it all begins with setting up meaningful public and private Social Media communities that are monitored and filtered to generate social insight for integration into customer profiles/Social CRM systems for use in customer engagement activities.

## Social Media Strategy Process

The three stages an organization must undertake to design a best-in-class Social Media strategy are contemplate, navigate, and calibrate.

### Contemplate

The key steps within the contemplate stage are as follows:

1. Assess the current situation.
2. Understand the community's linkage to the overall business strategy.
3. Define the audience.
4. Determine the organization's Social Media goals.
5. Define/review the organization's Social Media policies.
6. Leverage organizational resources, such as SMEs.

The order of these steps is important. For example, the audience must be defined (Step 3) before the organization can determine Social Media goals (Step 4).

### Assess the Current Situation

In assessing the current situation, here are some key questions to consider:

- What Social Media efforts have taken place to date? Have they been successful? Who has the audience been?

- Who is the executive sponsor? If there is no executive sponsor, it will be a great deal harder to create a successful Social Media community.

- What are the business drivers behind the Social Media community?

- Are there multiple stakeholders who will be involved in the community, and are they on board?

### Understand the Community's Linkage to the Overall Business Strategy

Next, the organization must determine how the community will support the overall business strategy. Does the overall business strategy include enhancing internal collaboration (in which case a knowledge management community will play an important role)? Or does the overall business strategy focus on sales growth, new product development, superior customer service, or creating customer evangelists (in which case an external Social Media community will play an important role)? Needless to say, the tighter the link between the Social Media community and the overall business strategy, the more likely the organization will support the Social Media strategy and resulting Social Media communities.

### Define the Audience

It is important for the organization to determine which constituencies are the most appropriate for the emerging Social Media strategy and resulting Social Media communities. Will the community target employees, distributors, partners, customers, prospects, or others?

The organization will eventually want to perform technographic profiles for the selected audience because, as noted in the Front Runner case study (Chapter 3, "Social Media Pilot Case Study"), these profiles will reveal a lot more about the digital behavior of each potential audience member. These profiles include the following:

- What kinds of activities does the audience member like to do on the Internet?
- Which Social Media sites does the audience member frequent? What are the personalities of these sites?

The objectives are to determine how best to court these individuals to come to the organization's Social Media community and to leverage feasible knowledge from their technographic profiles to help increase the likelihood of a successful community.

### Determine the Key Social Media Goals

Determining the key Social Media goals answers the following question: What is to be accomplished with the audience of the Social Media community? Chapter 5, "Creating Your Social Media Community in Support of Social CRM," described the ten key reasons for organizations to create a Social Media community; here are several Social Media goals that an organization can reasonably expect to achieve by creating a Social Media community:

- Increase collaboration (relevant for external communities and particularly relevant for an internal community).
- Increase customer engagement, satisfaction, loyalty, and advocacy (the three primary motivations of community members).
- Achieve satisfaction through the association with brand-oriented content.
- Create shared relationships, experiences, and viewpoints of peer members.
- Gain insight on how to make the business better.
- Gather information on topics and technology that help the organization's employees do their jobs better.
- Create opportunities to use the community for promotions.
- Promote exclusive branded merchandise.
- Increase revenue by
  - strengthening the brand,

- promoting the organization's products/services through word-of-mouth, and

- developing client evangelists.

- Decrease costs by

  - lowering customer support cost/service provision costs through self-service and community support,

  - determining best practices via communications tools offered in a community (blogs, forums, contests, and so on), and

  - decreasing acquisition costs (for example, using Social Media communities to attract prospects by introducing them to existing customers participating in the community).

### Define and Review the Social Media Policies

After defining the audience and determining the Social Media goals for the community, the next step in formulating a Social Media strategy is to define and review the organization's Social Media policies. These policies are used by the organization to protect its own interests, to promote its Social Media community goals, and to enhance usage of the community by its members. (Social Media policies are discussed in greater detail in Chapter 18, "Social CRM Technology Issues.")

### Leverage Organizational Resources

The organization next must ask what resources it has that can be leveraged to deliver the strategy. For an external Social Media community, organizational resources typically include SMEs who share insight in the form of a blog or an "Ask the Expert" forum. Organizational resources also may include providing community members with access to the organization's business partners, or even access to other customers.

## Navigate

In the navigate stage of a Social Media strategy, the organization must take the following steps:

1. Select the appropriate Social Media software vendor tools.

2. Define process flows.

3. Create an engagement plan.

### Select the Social Media Software Vendor Tools

When an organization is selecting the appropriate Social Media software vendor tools, it is important to consider which tools are capable of delivering on the organization's Social Media strategy. There is no shortage of Social CRM vendors or Social Media platform vendors that would like to establish themselves as a leading vendor in the Social CRM application space. Yet, there are meaningful differences between these vendors' applications regarding how intuitive and easy it is to navigate through the community, as well as whether their applications provide the functionality desired by community members. Appendix C, "Leading Social CRM Software Solutions," describes leading software vendor tools. Most of these tools deliver Social Media communities as a Cloud service, thus minimizing the burden on the organization's internal IT staff.

### Define Process Flows

Process flow addresses these two questions: Is navigation within the community intuitive to the user? And, what process flows are built into the community's navigation to ensure that community goals are met? For example, is the navigation flow within the community such that members will easily get answers to their questions from other members or SMEs, or that members will be motivated to become community evangelists?

When I worked with a prominent NYC-based publishing firm to create its Social Media strategy, the Social Media goals were to increase awareness and revenue by driving prospective customers to a point of sale on the organization's website. These goals were met by setting up required navigation on the Social Media communities—the company had multiple communities for each book genre. The publishing firm used two process flows to meet these goals:

- **Hub-and-spoke flows**—Each of the publishing firm's Social Media communities was designed to help drive traffic to the firm's website, where the visitor could access relevant information pertaining to a particular book or author of interest, and could ultimately purchase the desired book.

- **Clickstream flows**—The publishing company used clickstream flows to drive traffic from public Social Media communities to the firm's website, and also from the firm's website to its own Social

Media genre communities. More specifically, the firm's Social Media communities' home pages were set up as the click-through focal point to various Social Media communities and websites, and vice versa. For example, visitors who went to the firm's Facebook/ Twitter account, to the website, or to the partners' web pages, or who received emails/e-newsletters or advertising campaign materials, would click a URL that brought them directly to the firm's own Social Media communities, where community members (including publishing firm SMEs) could interact with them online. In turn, the communities' home pages also had links back to the firm's website and to external ecommerce sites, where the visitors could easily purchase books published by the firm.

Unfortunately many organizations formulating a Social Media strategy often overlook the importance of setting up meaningful process flows. A large number of Social Media communities have underperformed as a result.

### Create an Engagement Plan

The community-engagement plan is a critical document that describes how the organization will attract potential members to the Social Media community and keep them as members. The plan typically includes promoting the community on the organization's website home page, along with sending email notifications announcing the Social Media community to the organization's customers and prospects. To help secure traffic, the engagement plan should also contain links to the organization's Social Media community from other online publications, including partner publications and related public relations efforts. Many organizations also use *content seeding,* which is the use of ad words, online ads, contests, and links from other websites to drive traffic to their Social Media community. Once in the community, members need to find compelling content to keep them involved, which is another part of the engagement plan.

In a new global private Social Media community that I had the pleasure to design, the engagement plan played a critical role in securing customers and partners to join the community. The plan needed to create engagement materials in multiple languages, and when implementing activities noted in the engagement plan, the organization also had to be careful to adhere to local country/regional laws regarding data privacy. I am pleased to say that this new community is not only up and running, but also has already exceeded expectations as a result of following the plan.

## Calibrate

To calibrate an organization's Social Media strategy, one must set and measure community metrics, outline execution and ongoing support activities, and have a process to assess results and make improvements to the Social Media community. Each of these areas has its set of challenges.

### Setting and Measuring Metrics

Setting metrics is relatively simple, but measuring metrics is often challenging. It is hard to determine whether the lift in a member's sales resulted directly from participation in the community (causation) or if the community participation was just another factor that led to increased member sales (correlation). My advice: Organizations need to use multiple measurement tools, including online surveys, over a period of time to secure accurate community metrics.

Community metrics typically include community health and business metrics. Here are some of the better-known metrics in each category:

- **Community health metrics**—These metrics are straightforward, measure member activity/engagement in the community, and take time to achieve:
  - **Growth in participation**—Registered members, number of new members since inception of the community, followers, fans, and so on
  - **Growth in content**—Number of posts attached to each blog or forum
  - **Growth in traffic**—Page views
  - **Responsiveness**—Amount of time between a post and the first reply
  - **Topic interaction**—Number of posts per thread
  - **Engagement**—Level of activity (for example, how often do they visit the community, and how long do they stay?)

- **Business metrics**—These metrics are more difficult to quantify, but are as important as community health metrics. Business metrics help secure the ongoing support for the community from an organization's executives:

  - Increased revenue

  - Improved customer satisfaction and loyalty

  - Cost avoidance or reduction (for example, how much money was saved due to using the community to respond to customer service issues rather than sending these issues to contact center personnel?)

  - Better products and services resulting from ideas generated in the community

  - Higher brand recognition and related business profile metrics

### Ongoing Support Activities

To properly execute a Social Media strategy, an organization must have enough personnel to deliver all the elements required for a successful Social Media community. This is no small task. In Chapter 5, I discussed the importance of a governance structure for the Social Media community. One of the items that members of the governance structure are responsible for is securing ongoing support activities for the community, including the following:

- **Content creation**—Who is writing blogs, creating videos, and managing the forums?

- **Marketing**—Who is promoting the Social Media community?

- **Community management**—Who is managing the Social Media community?

- **Moderation**—Who is moderating the Social Media community?

- **Evaluation**—Who is evaluating the success of the Social Media community and ensuring that it is meeting its stated goals?

I opened Part IV, "Social CRM—Process Issues," with an acknowledgement that within the Social CRM people/process/technology mix, the process component is the most delicate aspect, because automating a broken Social CRM process will only make the process worse quicker. Many organizations embarking on the Social Media component of their

Social CRM initiatives have found the "contemplate, navigate, and calibrate" process framework valuable in creating a sound Social Media strategy.

In Part V, "Social CRM—People Issues," each of the three chapters will examine a people topic, including the importance of excellent communications throughout the Social CRM initiative, the different types of Social CRM training, and how to apply best people practices to the Social Media component of Social CRM.

# Part V
## Social CRM—People Issues

# 15

## Overcoming Inevitable People Issues

Of the three components discussed in Chapter 11, "Social CRM: Achieving the Right Mix of People, Process, and Technology," mastering the people component of a Social CRM implementation is the most difficult challenge for any organization, given the sensitivity of users to change. The following are three examples of Social CRM implementations I have been involved in where people issues were not managed properly, thus leading to the implementations' derailment, as well as two additional examples of where people issues were well handled, thus helping secure very successful implementations.

## Social CRM Implementation Failures

Here are three interesting examples of Social CRM implementation failures caused by the mismanagement of "people" issues, thereby leading the Social CRM implementation effort to break down. I present examples in the oil, telecom, and services industries.

### Oil Industry Failure

When a global player in the oil industry embarked on a Social CRM initiative, it established a superuser group comprising ten employees. The executive sponsor was a charming individual who had been with the organization for more than 35 years. He definitely saw the value of the Social CRM initiative, which included an internal-collaboration Social Media community, and he had many creative, valuable insights to help ensure the success of the initiative. Unfortunately, the internal project manager and one of the superusers were not of the same quality or demeanor. The internal project manager, who was from the IT side of the house, was convinced that she knew which Social CRM software was best for the organization, and that gathering user needs via a structured process was a waste of time. Throughout the initiative she did her best to actively lobby other superusers to see her point of view. Each of them was trying to be respectful of the project manager's point of view, but many disagreed with her, which led to dissention within the team.

While the project manager situation was going on, one of the superusers decided that because his division already had installed basic CRM functionality, it could not wait for the team to deliver prioritized Social CRM business functionality. Rather—and despite this being a global, cross-divisional project—his division needed to go ahead of all the other divisions and immediately install Social CRM functionality that he had prioritized on his own. As I dug deeper into his claims and visited more users from his division, the CRM functionality that had been implemented in the division was being used sparsely at best, but users were afraid to say this to the superuser (who had a very strong personality).

The executive sponsor did try to mitigate these issues and provide guidance to the internal project manager and to the superuser. Then all hell broke loose when the executive sponsor announced to the team that he had been promoted and would be leaving the Social CRM project in 30 days. Within days there was an all-out war over who would take over the Social CRM initiative—the project manager made a play, as did the one superuser. Long story short, with a vacuum at the top and unmanageable infighting among team members, the Social CRM initiative came to a sudden and costly close.

*Lessons learned:* People issues play a critical role in every successful *and* unsuccessful Social CRM initiative. The moment that people issues begin to negatively impact the initiative, change needs to be made. In the case of this organization, the project manager and the superuser should have been replaced early on. Moreover, the executive sponsor should have taken the time to pick and groom his successor, regardless of the pressure he faced to move into his new job role.

### *Telecom Industry Failure*

An international telecommunications organization launched a global Social CRM initiative a few years ago that included the formation of a superuser group comprising 12 to 15 representatives from sales, marketing, customer service, and other customer-facing functions. This group, formed at the outset of the initiative, was responsible for helping to secure the prioritized business functional requirements and technical features for the initiative.

Senior executives had doubts about the organization's ability to meet the initiative's deadlines and made the decision not to communicate or actively promote the initiative to potential internal and external users until the implementation neared completion. As with virtually all complex initiatives involving people and technology, a number of minor glitches emerged early on. The glitches were eventually resolved, but the organization's rumor mill elevated these glitches to the level of major problems—even system killers. By the time the organization was ready to invite internal and external users for training on the Social CRM application, about half said they knew little about the initiative, and that from what little they did know they were not interested in participating. Many employees declined to accept the training that was offered. The initiative struggled along for four more months. In the end the telecom pulled the plug on the project, incurring a substantial financial loss.

*Lessons learned:* Launch a full-fledged communications program about the Social CRM initiative at the outset. Ensure that key personnel and users understand how the new system will impact their day-to-day work. Update them regularly on how the implementation is progressing to avoid surprises.

### Services Industry Failure

A leading services organization launched a global Social CRM initiative a few years ago, and formed a core team consisting of senior managers from technical, business, and training functions. Business users were not involved at the outset, because one senior manager felt she could speak on their behalf. This turned out to be a mistake. It was evident early on that the senior manager was out of touch with the needs of business users (and perhaps even saw these users as a threat to her next promotion). She refused to collaborate closely with users and, after a year and a large amount of money invested, the organization put the Social CRM initiative on hold until a reorganization, which included replacing the senior manager, could take place.

*Lessons learned:* Don't be afraid to let users drive the system's specifications and implementation.

## Social CRM Implementation Success Stories

Organizations can reap the benefits of Social CRM with an effort that emphasizes the involvement of all stakeholders in the implementation process. I now present two Social CRM implementation success stories in the publishing and raw materials industries.

## Publishing Industry Success Story

An international publishing organization established a superuser group to help launch its Social CRM initiative. This group remained active and engaged throughout the implementation, helping to select the Social CRM vendor software. More important, each superuser also took on a training role during the system launch to ensure that all users were on board throughout the initiative. In addition, the organization launched a comprehensive communications program at the outset that included issuing a weekly memo that updated potential internal and external users on the status of the initiative and scheduled question-and-answer sessions at key organizational meetings, including the organization's annual meeting, regional sales meetings, and customer service get-togethers. To the surprise of the executive sponsor, when training time for Social CRM applications came, an internal argument ensued between users and the training coordinator as to which users would get trained first. Almost all the users clamored to take part in the first training session because they couldn't wait to get their hands on the new system. All the users eventually were trained, and this Social CRM initiative continues to be a raving success.

*Lessons learned*: Get users involved early on, keep them informed throughout the initiative, and let them manage their own change.

## Raw Materials Industry Success Story

An international manufacturer to the raw materials industry launched its Social CRM initiative with great care and planning. The CEO and COO were 100 percent behind the initiative, which they felt was critical to achieve a better relationship with their global customers. The COO organized multiple learning sessions for the superuser group, which he flew at great expense into one location for each learning session. He also chose the director of sales operations as project manager, who was well liked by everyone in the organization. Although there were many differing opinions throughout the Social CRM initiative, including about prioritized business functionality and about which software vendor best met the organization's needs, the COO and director of sales operations stood side by side at each stage of the implementation to ensure that superusers' opinions were harmonized and that the organization moved forward in unison. Other than a few technical glitches resulting from the software vendor overpromising what its software could deliver, this Social CRM implementation went flawlessly and has tremendously impacted growth in sales, which was the key metric for this implementation.

*Lessons learned*: Ensure that there is strong executive support for the Social CRM initiative, nurture it well, and have the Social CRM initiative linked to the strategic direction of the organization. The Social CRM implementation effort should additionally be measured with key metrics on a regular basis to determine its rate of success.

## How to Secure People Success for a Social CRM Initiative

Here are five ways to help every organization address and overcome the inevitable people issues that challenge every Social CRM initiative:

- Announce Social CRM efforts internally
- Create a superuser group
- Create a meaningful communications program
- Keep the executive sponsor(s) actively engaged
- Maintain a long-term view

### Announce Social CRM Efforts Internally

The launch of a Social CRM initiative should be done with great pride and care. Many people in the organization will be curious to know about the initiative. Expect questions such as the following:

- Will I be included in the initiative?
- Who was selected to participate in the initiative and what were the selection criteria?
- How many people are included in the initiative?
- How long will the initiative last?
- How quickly will the initiative spread to members outside the initial user group?
- What will people participating in the user group need to do?
- Will my job change as a result of the initiative?

Carefully prepare answers to each question because it is important to ensure the Social CRM initiative gets off to a healthy start and that questions get answered early on.

The importance of internal communications cannot be overstated. I guided a Social CRM software-selection project for a U.S. manufacturer of industrial pipes. In this case, the Social CRM project leader was overly secretive about the project, and this created some misunderstandings among his colleagues associated with the project. As a result, several people decided either to tune out or discontinue participating in the ongoing project.

## Create a Superuser Group

Businesses must ensure that the project manager—responsible for coordinating all aspects of Social CRM project design and implementation—is solidly behind the initiative. Additionally, there should be an executive champion, who will be the highest-ranking executive willing to promote the Social CRM initiative in the organization and prevent bureaucratic obstacles from getting in the way of success. The Social CRM initiative should also be supported by a group of superusers (frontline personnel from sales, marketing, and customer service functions) to represent the voice of the user. The group should include representative individuals who are leaders among the best in their respective job functions and have a strong knowledge of the business.

The superusers are responsible for participating in key project events (from the brainstorming session) in business process enhancement work, during the software selection phase and throughout the specification/ design/implementation stages of the Social CRM initiative. Typically the superusers need to devote up to five days of their time throughout the initial two to four months of the Social CRM initiative, although this often is adjusted based on the length of Social CRM initiative, responsibilities of members of the superuser group, and so on. After the initial two to four months, the level of participation usually decreases considerably.

Superuser groups typically include the following members:

- The project manager
- At least one member of the IT department
- Frontline sales, marketing, and customer service personnel (including ebusiness and personnel responsible for looking after Social Media)

- At least one manager from one of the aforementioned departments
- Possibly someone from finance
- A channel partner representative if the organization sells products through partners

In another Social CRM success story, the project manager of a leading U.S. financial institution selected his superuser group and carefully monitored the team during the project initiation, design, and implementation. The value of this successful group paid for itself many times over when project disputes and disagreements—normal occurrences in every Social CRM project—were quickly resolved and the project moved forward with few interruptions.

### *Create a Meaningful Communications Program*

Once the Social CRM initiative has been announced in the organization and the project manager and superuser group have been selected, the next step is to set up a communications program that focuses on communicating effectively on an on-going basis with all members of the Social CRM initiative. Open and constructive communications are paramount to keep the executive sponsor, project manager, superuser-group members, IT department, and any consultants or vendors working on the project up to speed on what is transpiring and when. The organization may want to ensure that customers are kept aware of the Social CRM initiative and how it will impact them.

Remember, organizational personnel will talk about the Social CRM project, so it is important to send a continuous stream of information to build ongoing internal support and enthusiasm for the initiative, while keeping all parties up to date on activities in which they will be involved (participating in the brainstorming session, helping to enhance a business process, and so on). Watch for any signs of an internal rumor-mill funneling inaccurate information that would limit participation and hinder the long-term success of the project.

There are two basic types of Social CRM project communications:

- **Strategic communications**—Typically these are messages from top executives explaining why the Social CRM initiative is important to the organization, as well as stories about how other organizations within and outside of the organization's industry have successfully implemented Social CRM initiatives, and how they have benefited from these initiatives.

- **Tactical communications**—Typically these are specific communications about an activity taking place or that has been completed in the Social CRM initiative (governance structure setup, Social CRM vendor finalists selected, business process improvement team formed, and so on). They also can be individual specific (for example, "You are requested to participate in the Social CRM Awareness learning session at 2:30 p.m. next Wednesday.").

Many organizations use the following vehicles for sending strategic and/or tactical communications:

- A web page or a section on the organization's intranet
- Emails or updates on Social Media communities
- Internal Social Media collaboration community
- Articles in specific communication departmental vehicles (for example, internal newsletters and periodicals)
- Presentations at organizational special events (for example, sales meetings and regional meetings)
- Social CRM project status updates at departmental executive meetings
- Executive videos
- Town hall meetings to discuss Social CRM issues and/or the organization's Social CRM project status

Managing communications effectively becomes more important if the Social CRM project is implemented in more than one region or country. In this case, keeping potential superusers and all other users within other regions or countries informed about current Social CRM efforts becomes vital, because this helps pave the way for a smoother transition as the system expands from one set of users to the next. Managing communications in one international project translated into setting up quarterly review meetings with designated personnel from 12 European countries. The benefit of these meetings was clear: The project was rolled out across Europe with minimal difficulty and maximal country participation.

*An observation:* It is not possible to over-communicate during a Social CRM initiative.

## Keep the Executive Sponsor(s) Actively Engaged

Initial support from senior executives for the Social CRM project tends to be quite high. The key is to secure an executive sponsor early on who promotes the initiative to executive colleagues. Once this project champion is selected, request assistance from this individual as needed. Help the sponsor to create a buzz about its importance and expected impact. Keep the sponsor briefed every month for at least the first six months of the project, and quarterly thereafter. Briefings should be confined to one page of written bullet points (include progress and setbacks). Try to follow up with face-to-face meetings at least every quarter to maintain an open discussion on progress and setbacks regarding the Social CRM initiative.

Unfortunately, other issues and priorities can quickly consume the attention of your executive sponsor (remember the oil-industry failure story?). Be firm about holding briefings with the sponsor on a regular basis. Otherwise, there's a risk of losing the sponsor to other, more aggressive initiatives being promoted within the organization. Lack of senior executive support is a sure way to bring a project to a premature end. In one example, an organization's executive sponsor lost interest in the initiative and failed to provide bureaucratic support when it was needed. The initiative died within three months.

For another Social CRM project, the organization agreed to set up a four-person executive sponsorship group comprising the EVP and VPs of sales and marketing in the three global regions where the organization did business. When the executive sponsor was too busy, the VP for that region stepped in with full authority to act on the sponsor's behalf.

If possible, demonstrate the Social CRM system as it evolves to the executive sponsor. Of course, make sure the system works flawlessly. Executives talk with one other on a regular basis. Good news travels quickly at this level, which can add potential support to the Social CRM initiative.

## Maintain a Long-term View

Last, encourage all participants (the sponsor, users, stakeholders, customers, and so on) to maintain a long-term view during the Social CRM project and to be prepared to survive the project's growing pains. Overcoming a failure or two during project implementation often strengthens resolve and demonstrates to all that the project has needed user commitment and committed resources. I have been involved in many Social

CRM projects that have hit snags. Maintaining a long-term view will help diffuse and resolve most of these situations.

If the organization utilizes these five ways to address and hopefully overcome the inevitable people issues that challenge every Social CRM initiative, the chances for project success improve significantly. After all, people create Social CRM systems, and people use these systems. It is important to remain highly sensitive to the strengths and weaknesses of users and to work diplomatically within the boundaries set by these individuals.

In the next chapter, I turn to the crucial people component of effective Social CRM training.

# 16

## Keeping Users Engaged and Happy

The following three components are required to ensure high user adoption of Social CRM systems and happy and engaged users:

- Effective training
- A responsive help desk
- Comprehensive systems administration

These three components often determine the long-term success of any Social CRM implementation.

## Effective Training

Based on data ISM has compiled over the past 30 years, I have concluded that for every $1 spent on Social CRM technology (including hardware, software, communications equipment, and services), $1.50 should be budgeted for training over the lifespan of the project. In other words, if a customer spends $500,000 on technology, approximately $750,000 should be allocated for training costs over the life of the project (typically, five years). A greater percentage of training money typically is allocated to the first year of the project to cover business-process training and application training, so rather than 20 percent of the budget allocated for each of the five years, it is more like 40 percent in year one and 15 percent in the remaining four years. Multiple types of training are needed for a successful Social CRM implementation, as discussed next.

### Business-Process Training

As noted in Part IV, "Social CRM—Process Issues," many different business processes go into a successful Social CRM system, including sales, marketing, customer service processes, and Social Media processes.

It will be necessary to train users on each of these new processes, whether the process is new or enhanced. I like to bring users together and present how to use the new or enhanced business process within in multiple, real-life business scenarios.

Social Media process training is by far the most challenging area of Social CRM business-process training. Chapter 5, "Creating Your Social Media Community in Support of Social CRM," described the many challenges associated with successful realization of the Social CRM framework. The process of training the appropriate users how to monitor and filter information, how to take the resulting social insight and integrate it into customer profiles or elsewhere in the Social CRM system, and then how to use the social insight in the customer engagement process is not intuitive to all. This training is critical because if social insight is not leveraged in the customer engagement process, the full impact of Social CRM will not be realized.

## Application Training

Application training typically consists of face-to-face training sessions held at the organization's facilities, at the vendor's facilities, or at a third-party site. Some vendors, especially those providing Cloud or web-based software applications, increasingly offer online training using collaboration tools and services that run on in-house or on outsourced learning management systems. Training can be done in-house or purchased from the software vendor, from the implementation firm if one is used, or from specialty training companies. Each approach has its pros and cons in terms of costs, resource requirements, and so on.

Hands-on Social CRM application-training sessions tend to last between one and two days, although sessions may run shorter or longer, depending on the system's complexity. Optimal training has between eight and 12 user participants attending each face-to-face training session. Ideally, the instructor-to-student ratio does not exceed one to six, meaning at least one instructor for every six students. I like the room to be set up with an instructor at the front of the room teaching and another instructor at the back of the room making sure that participants are keeping up and assisting participants as needed. For optimal results, it is best not to exceed 15 participants in any one training session.

These sessions should include hands-on training whereby participants have PCs, laptops, tablets, or other handheld devices with Internet access. This way, as the instructor explains a function or feature, participants can immediately perform that function on their devices. Best practice is to have an instructor script prepared to ensure the training is tightly linked to the organization's Social CRM business processes.

Each application-training session should provide users with an overview of the system by offering "a day in the life of" training, then go into individual system functions and features. It's important to ensure that participants take a hands-on test after each training section to show that they have understood how to effectively put to use what was taught in that section. Some organizations have computer-based training programs that automatically score the user's test results. Each participant also should receive during the training session a set of quick reference cards on the Social CRM system. Some organizations also hand out a CD to participants containing a more comprehensive User Guide.

### Train-the-Trainer

This type of training is used when an organization prefers to do its own training or in cases where there are so many users that it would be unrealistic to train them all at once. The software vendor or a third-party specialized-training company typically teaches the initial train-the-trainer session. The participants of this session are the organization's internal trainers who need to learn how to use the system so they in turn can teach other users. This session should follow the same format as the application training (that is, one to two days long), but each trainer should also be provided with a training manual to implement user training with excellence. Train-the-trainer has some advantages and disadvantages. The key advantage is having an internally controllable, cost-effective means to train a large number of organizational personnel. The key disadvantage is being dependent on in-house organizational trainers. If these individuals are busy with other assignments, this may delay the training of users on the Social CRM system.

### Systems Administrator Training

The Social CRM software vendor typically offers this training. This specialized training takes place between the vendor's trainers and the organization's assigned systems administrators. The training's objective is to teach the systems administrators how to perform day-to-day system maintenance such as assigning passwords, customizing system fields and screens, updating databases, integrating social insight into customer pro-files/elsewhere in the CRM system, and other related areas.

System administrator training typically takes between one and three days to complete. Again, the training should be hands on, with a ratio that should not exceed one instructor for every three participants. Each systems administrator should also receive comprehensive system docu-mentation during the training session.

Moderators of the Social Media community need a specialized train-ing session, during which the moderator learns how to sign up new mem-bers to the community, how to delete user posts to the community that violate community policies, how to break up a forum tread into multiple threads, how to create community metrics, and so on. This session typi-cally lasts one day.

### Remedial Training

Individuals trained on the system and who use the system soon after training are likely to retain much of their training. But even the most sea-soned learner can benefit from periodic remedial training updates, par-ticularly if there are updates to the software, including new functions and features. Remedial training sessions should be scheduled within three to six months after the system has been implemented and done at least annually thereafter. Remedial training can be done using e-learning and Internet/web-based online training. Ask the software vendor or third-party training specialists what remedial training they offer.

### New User Training

All too often, organizations forget to set up new-user training, which should be done every three or so months. Some organizations like new users to learn the ropes from existing users, but I have not found this to be an effective way to ensure that the new user master the Social CRM software application. In fact, in most companies that have low Social CRM user adoption, the root cause is often a failure to train now users properly.

*Closing observation:* Never underestimate the importance of train-ing to a Social CRM project's overall success. There is no such thing as overtraining on a Social CRM system. Too much training is not enough; more is better.

# A Responsive Help Desk

Every Social CRM system user should have access from within the application to a comprehensive, online help function. Complementing the online help function should be an internal help desk set up for Social CRM users that takes questions by phone, email, text message, via the Web, or via Social Media. Some organizations use a third-party help desk, but this requires that the third-party be well trained on the Social CRM application.

The help desk fulfills several important needs, including one phone number or one URL to contact when the user encounters a problem. The help desk should be staffed with properly trained personnel and supported by help desk software described in this chapter. In smaller organizations, the help desk can be integrated with the systems administrator function. In larger organizations, the employees are usually trained to support Social CRM applications only or trained to support multiple applications within the organization, including the Social CRM application.

A successful help desk requires that strict business procedures be followed when handling incoming questions. For example, each question received must be logged into a help desk software program so that there is a record of all incoming questions. When a user's question cannot be answered on the spot (first-call resolution), the help desk should then route the question to the appropriate individual within the organization to a second support tier, such as the systems administrator, who in turn tracks the user question until it gets resolved. In the worst-case scenario, a question may require changes in software code, which may mean that the help desk will need to route the question to the organization's IT department or even to the software vendors for what is referred to as third-tier support.

Regardless of the type of question received and its routing procedure, the question must be logged into the help desk's tracking system once the user's question has been resolved. A summary of how long the resolution process took and of the solution to the question should be captured in a knowledge base for future reuse by others. Reports generated from help desk information are used to improve help desk functioning and to prioritize training needs or system alterations and enhancements.

# Comprehensive Systems Administration

In most organizations, a systems administrator is required to manage the Social CRM system. Responsibilities of the systems administrator include the following:

- Ensure the system's data is kept up to date so that it is timely and relevant.
- Back up system files and data on a regular basis.
- Provide new users with IDs and passwords.
- Make changes to fields on the screen, in pull-down menus, and other minor customizations.
- Roll out software releases and updates.
- Create and/or report on system usage statistics.
- Report on problems that occur with the system.
- Write systems reports and implement related systems tasks (for example, workflow routines)

The systems administrator, typically with the help of the Social Media community moderator, is also responsible for logging in how many relevant comments concerning particular topics were monitored and filtered from the Social Media communities, and for sending this social insight into the correct customer profile or elsewhere within the Social CRM application.

Be sure to staff the systems administration function with qualified individuals. Customers, executives, customer-facing representatives, and field personnel who rely on the Social CRM system expect that it be a properly working one that contains up to date, accurate information.

Address early on the need for effective training, a responsive help desk, and comprehensive systems administration. Sadly, there are many Social CRM implementations now prematurely in the graveyard because of the organization's failure to realize the importance of these three components up front; they really do help to keep users engaged and happy.

In the next chapter, I specifically look at several of the people challenges typically encountered when creating the Social Media community piece of a Social CRM initiative.

# 17

## Applying "People" Best Practices to Social Media

Given the importance of getting the Social Media component right to deliver a successful Social CRM initiative, I focus this chapter on applying the best "people" practices related to an organization's Social Media effort. These best practices include the following:

- Creating and adhering to Social Media policies
- Developing realistic time estimates
- Enhancing motivation
- Leveraging passion

## Creating and Adhering to Social Media Policies

A best practice for an organization undertaking a Social CRM initiative is to invite employees to engage on a regular basis in the Social Media community, regardless of whether it is an internal or external community. This includes writing blogs, acting as an SME, participating in forums, and posting relevant comments to the community. To protect its interests and promote its Social Media goals, another best practice is for the organization to put into place Social Media policies that ensure employees properly participate in the community. Effective Social Media policies inform employees what they can and cannot do when it comes to participating in Social Media communities.

Organizations that have Social Media policies in place typically include at a minimum one policy for all employees and one only for employees who deal with Social Media in their job. An organization's Social Media policies should honor the organization's corporate values (for example, honesty, transparency, accuracy, and humility). In addition, these policies should clearly state that while employees work for the organization, the opinions they express are their own and do not represent those of the organization—unless the opinion comes from an official spokesperson. It is important for employees to understand that what is placed on Social Media communities is forever—just like what is placed on the Internet—and that deleting material is extremely difficult.

In addition to informing employees what they can and cannot do, good Social Media policies encourage employees to become social advocates for the organization. Every employer has employees who are enthusiastic, positive, and passionate about their work and the organization. The last thing an organization wants is to discourage these people from communicating their enthusiasm and knowledge in their Social Media participation (for example, posts). For example, I have a friend who is a General Motors employee and who is active on Facebook. This friend regularly posts links to positive General Motors press information on his Facebook page, and his links are always prefaced with a positive, sometimes personal statement.

The organization's Social Media policies should encourage employees to share their enthusiasm about their work and the organization, and to post/repost or to tweet/retweet good news about it. The organization should engage internal SMEs to blog, comment on blogs, and share their knowledge and expertise in a positive way. One important rule: Always identify employees in the Social Media community. This adds credibility to the organization and to the community.

It is also important to recognize employees' efforts to regularly make valuable comments or help to create buzz about the organization and its products/services. This can be done via special badging in the community, a pat on the back, or otherwise. If employees slip up, let them know privately and quickly. Adjust the Social Media policies if the situation warrants it. Last, because personality and expertise count more than title in a Social Media community, do not overlook the potential of getting all levels of employees involved in the community.

### Social Media Policy Recommendations

The following are three "best practices" components of a Social Media policy that every organization should keep in mind:

- **Legislate**—Social Media policies need to share with employees why the organization needs these policies, the process for setting up and amending Social Media policies, and how the organization contains risk while encouraging employees to be Social Media advocates.

- **Communicate**—Social Media policies need to describe clearly the process for communicating Social Media plans and strategies across the organization, to clients, and potentially to other stakeholders. Social Media is fast paced; therefore, effective, timely communication is important.

- **Energize**—Social Media policies should explain how Social Media can be used to energize employees, partners, and customers. Being heard on Social Media communities can provide meaningful fulfillment to an employee, partner, or customer.

A Social Media policy should not be just a laundry list of prohibitions. Instead, it should be seen by employees as a way to encourage them to be active in Social Media communities in ways that are beneficial to the organization. With this in mind, here are some Social Media policy recommendations:

- Encourage employees to join LinkedIn and to build their network of contacts; LinkedIn is an excellent way to network within and outside the organization.

- Ensure that executives also follow the organization's Social Media policies and actively participate in the community. Remember the adage, "what interests my boss fascinates me."

- Follow members of the executive team on Twitter and retweet their tweets as appropriate.

- "Like" the organization's Facebook page (very important).

- Encourage employees to join and actively participate in the organization's Social Media community. Their comments should be intelligent, insightful, and should reflect well on the organization.

Appendix A, "Social Media Policy Examples," provides three examples of excellent Social Media policies that have been successfully applied to organizations. Also consider going to www.socialmediagovernance. com, which is a valuable resource for Social Media policies.

# Developing Realistic Time Estimates

Nearly all organizations underestimate the time and effort required to deliver a successful Social Media program. Here are some examples:

- Setting up a content calendar for the community takes a lot of time and commitment from others. Do they have this time? Will they make this commitment?

- All bloggers will confirm that it always takes longer to write a blog post than initially anticipated. Writing a post takes approximately a half a day.

- Generating relevant content for the organization's Social Media community depends on the goals of the community and may require several writers with different expertise, styles, and viewpoints. This is the wildcard element that can throw off all time estimates.

- If employees are encouraged to monitor the Web and other Social Media communities for what others have said about the organization, determine how much time this will take and allot this time accordingly. This effort will likely take as much time as monitoring press clips, but remember that there is much more content to monitor on the Web and in Social Media communities.

- Allow appropriate time to repost and retweet materials such as blog entries, white papers, technical material, and so on.

- The community manager in most cases needs to allocate 15 to 40 hours per week, depending on the size and activities taking place within the community. Plan accordingly.

- Community monitoring is time-consuming and must be done with excellence. This can take anywhere from a couple of hours per day to 24/7 coverage.

As a rule of thumb, correlate time estimates to existing tasks. Also remember that a learning curve is associated with all these activities, so allocate an additional 15 to 20 percent to the time scheduled and beyond for what is needed to perform these activities. Most employees want to do an excellent job for the organization, so be realistic about the time estimated and allocate their time accordingly.

# Enhancing Motivation

It is important to understand what motivates top Social Media performers. One Federal Reserve Bank of Boston study conducted at MIT shows that for blue-collar workers who perform mechanical and rote tasks, more money will lead to better performance. However, for knowledge workers who conduct cognitive and complicated tasks such as actively participating in the organization's Social Media community, the study concluded that more money would not necessarily lead to better performance.[1]

Knowledge workers are more motivated by the following:

- **Autonomy or self-direction**—Twenty percent of a knowledge worker's time optimally is spent on what they desire to do.
- **Mastery**—Performing work they enjoy so much that they will get better at it.
- **Purpose**—The feeling that they are making a contribution.

*Observation:* Take the time to learn what is important to the key contributors of a community, and motivate them accordingly. Successful communities have found that employee rewards can play a significant role in helping to enhance motivation.

# Leveraging Passion

Here are some Social Media examples that were successful in leveraging passion: One organization challenged its interns to make 60-second videos about why the company was an excellent organization to work for as an intern. The interns spent hours making these videos, which were then placed on the organization's career website and on YouTube. This program was quite successful in creating original, compelling Social Media content for the organization. It also served to generate much relevant commentary on these videos from the viewers of the videos, which the organization in turn used for its own benefit.

Another example is one of the AAA clubs that we worked with on its Social Media community. This club has an automotive expert who enjoys posting within the AAA Social Media community. Because he is very knowledgeable and funny in his posts, he gets many questions posted for him in the community. He has since built a following in the Social Media community. It is a win-win for all: He loves posting on the community,

community members love reading his posts and asking him questions, and the AAA club has seen a meaningful lift in member engagement.

Still another example of leveraging passion is Dennis Smith, who created a presence in the Social Media arena due to his work in telecommunications. His blog eventually became one of the top 50 in the telecommunications industry.

The lesson learned from these examples? In any organization's Social Media effort, it is important to empower employees to build a strong Social Media presence, which when properly done will be of tremendous benefit to the organization and its customers.

In this chapter, I have described several "people" best practices related to the Social Media component of the Social CRM Framework. These include creating and adhering to Social Media policies, developing realistic time estimates, enhancing motivation, and leveraging passion. Remember that the people component accounts for 50 percent of the success of a Social CRM initiative. My advice: Involve employees, stakeholders, and customers early on the planning process; be realistic about setting timeframes; and be sure to meaningfully reward people who help drive Social CRM success. At the end of the day, people will make or break the organization's Social CRM initiative.

Part VI, "Social CRM—Technology Issues," covers technology issues, where I examine the role of technology in Social CRM, key technology trends that will impact Social CRM, and how to address security risks in a Social CRM initiative.

# Endnotes

1. Federal Reserve Bank of Boston, "Large Stakes and Big Mistakes," http://www.bostonfed.org/economic/wp/wp2005/wp0511.pdf (July 23, 2005).

# Part VI
# Social CRM—Technology Issues

# 18

## Social CRM Technology Issues

Process issues are the most delicate, people issues the greatest challenge, and technology issues the most complex in the people/process/technology mix. There is an ever-expanding number of Social CRM technical options in the marketplace. Here are the four technology issues I focus on in this chapter:

- Dealing with Social CRM software vendors
- Key technology challenges
- Social CRM technology trends
- Social CRM security risks

## Dealing with Social CRM Vendors

Two distinct software vendor camps are competing for Social CRM business: One is the leading Social Media platform vendors, which include Acquia, Bazaarvoice, Get Satisfaction, INgage Networks, Jive, Lithium, Mzinga, and Zimbra. These vendors created the Social Media platform tools used to create Social Media communities. The platforms offer functionality such as blogs, discussion forums, contests, polls, user-generated content management, community tracking, and so on. Around 2008, these vendors concluded that their standalone Social Media community offerings, which at the time were not tightly integrated with CRM functions such as the customer profile, had a limited runway for growth. Consequently, these vendors have been expanding—with varying degrees of success—their Social Media platforms to include CRM functionality and linkages into CRM functionality in the areas of sales, marketing, and customer service.

In the other camp are the CRM vendors that have made a major push into Social CRM over the past five or so years. These vendors include Aptean, Infor, Oracle, Salesforce.com, SAP, and update software AG. They realized that with the explosive growth in Social Media, and the increased value of social insight for managing customer relationships, they needed either to integrate with or create their own Social Media functionality (for example, social monitoring, filtering, and integration with Social Media platforms).

When an organization sets out to select the best software for its Social CRM initiative, the challenge is to determine which vendor camp best fits the organization's needs. The organization must ask these questions: "Can all the organization's Social CRM needs be met by one of the vendor camps? If not, is it feasible to select and integrate the best from each vendor camp so that the organization can achieve its Social CRM goals?"

An equally important question is, "Can either vendor camp actually deliver on all that it promises in its Social CRM software offering?" I have been in the CRM/Social CRM industry for 30 years and am a pragmatic individual. My response to this question is as follows: Given that the Social CRM industry is in the third inning of a new ballgame, the current answer is "maybe." The implication of this answer should be clear: Be extremely careful to conduct appropriate due diligence when dealing with Social CRM vendors. Let me share a couple of war stories regarding vendors not telling the full truth.

In one case, a leading Social CRM software vendor claimed its software seamlessly integrated with all Social Media platforms. While performing due diligence, I concluded that the integration was *not* seamless, and that it actually required a fairly expensive piece of middleware to connect the Social CRM software to the Social Media platform used by my customer.

In another case, the Social Media platform vendor claimed that it contained CRM functionality within its platform toolset, including a comprehensive customer profile. Upon further analysis, I concluded that although the platform vendor did indeed have a database that could store customer information, the platform did not contain the required workflow tools to allow for the creation of a meaningful customer profile that could add value in the organization's customer engagement efforts.

Perhaps my favorite story of all is this: One of the largest database software vendors claimed that its emerging Social CRM software offering would contain the most comprehensive Social CRM functionality in the industry. Quite a few potential buyers actually waited many months for the promised functionality to arrive. Finally, under pressure from a variety of sides, including analysts, the Social CRM vendor was forced to admit that it would not be able to offer the promised functionality.

The following are the lessons I have learned when dealing with Social CRM software vendors: For the most part, vendors are honest and they mean well. However, because of the fierce competition from other vendors and pressures from industry analysts, venture capitalists, and so on, they may be forced to stretch the truth from time to time. It is important to understand this and to make the vendor demonstrate its promises and solutions in real time. Do not give the vendor the opportunity to tell the organization why the "hammer fits the organization's nail." Rather, perform the structured approach in Chapter 9, "Social CRM Software Selection and Vendor Negotiation," and drive the software-selection process based on the ability of the software vendor to meet the organization's stated Social CRM needs.

## Key Technology Challenges

I have already introduced the key technology challenges, each of which takes place within the Social CRM framework described in Chapter 4, "Leverage Social Media Information to Advance Your Social CRM Efforts" (the framework picture is shown in Figure 18.1). These key challenges are summarized here.

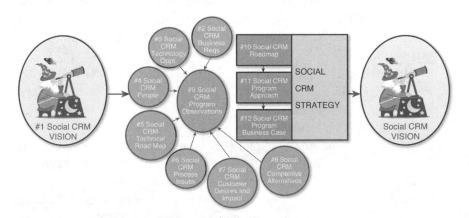

**Figure 18.1** The Social CRM framework

## Technology Challenge 1

This technology challenge involves Social Media monitoring and filtering (Steps 1 and 2 of the Social CRM framework).

Social Media monitoring is the process of following Social Media chatter about an organization, an organization's products/service, an industry, and so on. Social Media filtering describes how the monitoring tool utilizes rules-based filter searches on specific criteria, including, for example, a specified group of key customers or a comparison of brand sentiment for an organization compared to its competitors.

Both Social CRM vendor camps have entered the fray. In the CRM software camp, vendor Salesforce.com purchased Radian6. In the Social Media platform camp, vendor Lithium purchased Scout Labs. (Literally hundreds of monitoring and filtering tools are currently available. I expect to see a great deal of consolidation and acquisition of these tools by software vendors over the next five years as the Social Media monitoring industry matures. For a list of leading Social Media monitoring and filtering vendors, turn to Appendix B, "Leading Social Media Monitoring and Filtering Tools.")

## Technology Challenge 2

This technology challenge involves the integration of social insight into Social CRM customer profiles and elsewhere in the Social CRM system (Step 3 of the Social CRM framework).

The technology challenges of the integration of social insight will focus on the best way to technologically integrate the social insight gathered from public and private social communities, from blogs, and elsewhere on the Web. There are currently three ways to technically integrate social insight into a Social CRM application:

- Most vendors offer standard APIs to achieve this integration.
- Some vendors have created business process flows and programmed this social insight integration directly into their software platform.
- Other vendors have written software to reach out to filtered social insight and pull this insight into their Social CRM application.

Although both vendor camps are working on creating these integration tools, at this time there is no open standard for this critical integration piece of the Social CRM framework. As the Social CRM industry evolves, I see open integration standards being agreed on by both vendor camps that will make this integration so simple and intuitive that Social CRM users will be able to dictate what will be integrated into the Social CRM application.

## Technology Challenge 3

This technology challenge involves customer engagement (Step 4 of the Social CRM framework).

Customer engagement includes the process by which the organization leverages the social insight stored in the customer profile and elsewhere within the Social CRM application to engage with customers or prospects via their preferred channel(s). For example, if the customer opens the two-way dialogue with the organization via Twitter, the organization will want to initially respond back to the customer via Twitter. If the customer opens the two-way dialogue via the organization's private Social Media community, the organization will want to initially respond back to the customer via the community. This implies that there will be Social CRM software in place capable to receive and transmit all sorts of communications with the customer directly from the Social CRM tool. The technology being used by companies such as LiveOps and Salesforce.com are leading the pack in the area of customer engagement, but this technology challenge remains a work in progress.

Another part of the technology challenge associated with customer engagement is the availability of tools within Social CRM software to engage customers. These tools include Social Media communities, mobile apps, gamification, personalization, loyalty programs, contests, real-time decisioning, and more. I will discuss some of these topics in detail in Part VII, "The Future of Social CRM," but for now let me say that there is a great improvement in the number and quality of these tools being integrated at this time into the evolving Social CRM software. The future looks bright.

Here is an example of effective customer engagement in action coming from one of my customers: This global publishing organization has created multiple Social Media communities by genre (science fiction, mysteries, romance, and so on) for its book fans. If a customer shows an interest in a community topic, the organization uses the personalization tools contained within its Social CRM application to send a personalized message to the customer via the community, or in some cases via an email inviting customers, for example, to meet with their favorite author or to receive advance chapters from the author's next book. The customer response rate to these personalized messages has been astounding.

Despite this not being a technology challenge, I would be remiss not say, as I discussed in Chapter 5, "Creating Your Social Media Community in Support of Social CRM," that while having integrated social insight available for customer engagement purposes is clearly beneficial, knowing how best for employees to use this insight during the customer engagement process remains a work in progress.

## Social CRM Technology Trends

Staying on top of Social CRM technology trends has become increasingly difficult because of the proliferation of Social CRM technologies offered in the marketplace. Rather than trying to keep up with each new technology, organizations should track major technology developments that are most likely to impact the Social CRM industry's future and their own organizational Social CRM efforts.

Appendix D, "Social CRM Technology Trends," goes into additional detail regarding each of the following seven major technology trends that are currently impacting the technical evolution of Social CRM, and which should be taken into account when selecting a Social CRM application:

- Client/server architecture enhancements
- XML playing a major role in Social CRM
- Social CRM vendors including more portal architecture
- Growing options for filtering/exporting relevant Social Media community information
- Social CRM vendors incorporating business intelligence
- Social CRM vendors associating themselves with Resource Oriented Architecture (ROA)
- Growing options in licensing/hosting Social CRM

## Social CRM Security Risks

The growth of Social CRM is exposing organizations to more risk than ever before. Social Media communities open the organization to all kinds of new exposure. There is additional risk coming from other components of Social CRM technology, including hardware, software, operating systems, middleware, and networks. Minimizing security risk for Social CRM is similar to other applications that leverage the Internet: The organization must create a security culture and then provide the tools to reduce security risks. To learn more about Social CRM security risk, turn to Appendix E, "Addressing Social CRM Security Risks."

This chapter concludes the technology section of the book. I have discussed in detail two technology issues: dealing with Social CRM software vendors and key technology challenges that take place within the Social CRM framework. I have also introduced two additional technology issues: Social CRM technology trends and Social CRM security risks, which are explored in greater detail in the appendixes. I'll close with an observation. In the past few years there have been a lot of acquisitions and mergers in the Social CRM technology space. This has already led to some consolidation of technologies, and I expect to see more consolidations in the future.

Therefore, as an organization evaluates Social CRM solutions, it needs to pay careful attention to how tightly integrated the Social CRM vendor's software modules actually are. When evaluating Social CRM technology, focus on the Social CRM vendor holistically rather than only on its product/service offering. The vendor's technology may be "hot," but more important, does the vendor have the resources and experience to deliver the technology to support the organization's Social CRM system requirements and schedule? Remember that for a successful Social CRM initiative, technology accounts for no more than 20 percent of the overall success of a Social CRM initiative, with people accounting for at least 50 percent and processes for at least 30 percent.

In Part VII, I discuss the impact on Social CRM of six trends: the customer of the future, mobility, gamification, Big Data analytics and insight, channel optimization, and the Internet of Things.

# Part VII
## The Future of Social CRM

# 19

## Customers of the Future and Their Impact on Social CRM

The impact of the customer of the future on Social Media will be quite profound. There are more than 2 billion people using Social Media worldwide.[1] Facebook members alone exceed 1.35 billion members, of which 864 billion use Facebook daily.[2] Among U.S. adults, 74 percent use Social Media daily, and 89 percent of millennials use Social Media daily.[3] The Social Media phenomenon is not going away—it will continue to impact both the customer of the future and, in turn, the future of Social CRM.

As the worldwide population increasingly adopts Social Media, organizations must ask, "Can we afford not to connect with potential customers in the way that they expect to be communicated with?" My forecast is very simple: Social Media will meaningfully change the way that organizations market, sell, and service their customers. Opening a two-way dialogue with customers is no longer an option but a necessity for the organization to survive.

These surviving organizations will master the integration of each customer's emotional/sentiment needs, which has its roots in gathering social insight about the customer from Social Media communities, with existing transactional customer information (what the customer has purchased in the past, the profitability of the customer, and so on) to provide a more complete understanding of how best to market to, sell to, and service the customer of the future. The following is an example of how an organization should deal with the customer of the future.

## Happy Hotels: Debbie Jones Case Study

Let's look at what Debbie Jones, a customer of the future, has been up to. As owner of the Happy Hotels chain, I can use my Social CRM system to easily look at information concerning Debbie's activities at our hotels, including the following:

- **Transactional information** coming from our back-office systems, such as how many stays Debbie has per year, average amount spent during each stay, loyalty program membership status, onsite requests, settlement type, room type, any preferred onsite activities, her activities on Happy Hotels' website, and so on.

- **Demographic, behavioral, and lifestyle data** about Debbie gathered using third-party data overlays from companies such as Acxiom, Experian, and so on. This information includes marital status, number of children, home ownership status, types of cars driven, VIP level memberships, program loyalty levels, recent job changes, Web and Social Media usage, and more.

As owner of Happy Hotels, I am also able to obtain pertinent information on what is called Debbie's *social graph*, which is gathered from Facebook and other Social Media communities that she belongs to (Debbie does not appear to have any issues sharing this data with others and therefore has not put any data privacy constraints on her Social Media accounts). I am able to gather Debbie's social graph, which includes Facebook profile information, number of Facebook friends, Facebook likes, Facebook wants, key items she would like to own, what her Facebook friends like, and so on. Debbie's social graph confirms, for example, that she is a fan of the Happy Hotels chain, she loves the Happy Hotels lounge bars, she is a jogger, she is a member of Kids Club, she wants to purchase a new house with an attractive mortgage rate, and she dislikes when telemarketers call her on the phone. A social graph displays connection points between Debbie in this case and other people, places, and things that she interacts with online. Debbie's social graph is the representation of her relationships online and can provide for a robust analysis of her Social Media activities.

I am now ready to integrate the social insight information from Debbie's social graph directly into Debbie's customer profile that is currently housed within Happy Hotels' new Social CRM system. This puts Happy Hotels in a unique position to leverage Debbie's (1) transactional information, (2) demographic, behavioral, and lifestyle data, and (3) social graph data that has been harvested from multiple sources. This way, I can begin to engage with Debbie more effectively, whether it is from a marketing, sales, or service perspective.

I can even go a step further. In Debbie's Facebook profile, she discusses what she likes (for example, she has stayed at several Happy Hotel locations and loved her experience at each one). In addition, Debbie's friends also have stayed at various Happy Hotels locations and also loved their experience there. Subsequently, Debbie and her friends have had discussions in various Social Media communities about their Happy Hotels experiences. After monitoring and analyzing these discussions to generate relevant social insight information, Happy Hotels not only can engage with Debbie more knowledgeably, but also engage with Debbie's friends and potentially with all members of the Social Media communities that Debbie and her friends are members of.

In effect, my Happy Hotels' employees are in a unique position to leverage our Social CRM system—including, in this case, sales and marketing engagement tools—to more accurately target likely customers like Debbie and her friends and to make more relevant offers to these customers. We can promote our hotels via each customer's preferred channel, including Social Media, and we can make relevant offers such as, in Debbie's case, complimentary drinks at the Happy Hotels lounge or a weekend getaway for Debbie and two of her friends. This win-win situation helps drive Debbie's loyalty to and advocacy of Happy Hotels, and as a result Happy Hotels realizes additional revenues from Debbie and her circle of friends.

## Leveraging Social Graph Tools

In addition, Happy Hotels purchased 8thBridge, a social graph tool that we configured to drive customer loyalty and advocacy. Using the tool, we added new social graph buttons to our Happy Hotels website that go beyond the standard Facebook "Like" button. We decided to add new social graph data buttons, including "Joined," "Stayed," and "Love."

Here is how the new social graph buttons works: When Debbie next visits the Happy Hotels website and clicks, for example, the "Love" social graph button located on the website, she receives a thank-you notification via Facebook from Happy Hotels. It says, "Thanks Debbie for clicking our 'Love' Social Graph button, and also your most recent stay at our Happy Hotels location in *Name of City*." Shortly thereafter, Debbie's Facebook account receives a request from Happy Hotels asking for her thoughts regarding Happy Hotels' new Social Media program, as well as the relevancy of the recent offers that we have specifically targeted toward her stated interests. Once Debbie has opened this two-way dialogue with Happy Hotels, her Facebook friends can now also see what content she has downloaded from the Happy Hotels website, along with any special offers that she has received from Happy Hotels. Debbie begins to serve as an advocate for the Happy Hotels chain within the Social Media communities that she and her friends actively participate in.

Debbie can also post notice of all her Happy Hotels activities (for example, the dates and other details concerning her bookings) on her Facebook account. Debbie's friends, in turn, can access this timeline and "like" or comment on any of Debbie's Happy Hotels activities. Debbie and her friends can also access the same Happy Hotels' newsfeeds that offer promotions, as well as Happy Hotels' running ticker, which contains the latest news about activities at our hotels.

Relevant Social Media and social graph information about Debbie is automatically integrated into her customer profile within our Social CRM system for use in customer engagement activities. Using real-time decisioning tools that are a part of our Social CRM application, Happy Hotels is also able to present personalized offers to Debbie and her friends each time they visit Happy Hotels' website. In addition, feedback from social graph data and/or our website automatically becomes an input into our dynamic customer segmentation that we use for email marketing and Social Media marketing campaigns.

There is little wonder why our room occupancy rate has just surpassed 96 percent, why our revenues are up 12 percent, and why we have been notified that we will be receiving the coveted Most Creative Hotel Chain award from the prestigious Hotel Association of America. At Happy Hotels, we are proud that our investment in the new Social CRM system, with its extensive links into Social Media communities and tools, has meaningfully contributed to helping us lead the way in the competitive hotel industry.

*Key takeaway:* As seen in the Happy Hotels case study, the advent of Social CRM—inclusive of its extensive links to Social Media tools—has raised the bar by creating a two-way dialogue with the customer of the future. I am convinced, as a result, that the dynamics of the customer/ organization relationship have changed forever.

In the next chapter, I discuss another impact on Social CRM— namely that of mobility.

# Endnotes

1. We Are Social SG, "Social, Digital & Mobile in August 2014," http://wearesocial.sg/blog/2014/08/social-digital-mobile-august-2014/ (August 2014).

2. DMR Digital Marketing Ramblings, "By the Number: 200+ Amazing Facebook User Statistics," http://expandedramblings.com/index.php/by-the-numbers-17-amazing-facebook-stats/ (January 2, 2015).

3. Pew Research Center, "Social Networking Fact Sheet," http://www.pewinternet.org/fact-sheets/social-networking-fact-sheet/ (January 2015).

# 20

## The Impact of Mobility on Social CRM

Anyone with teenagers knows that the world's 1.7 billion millennials (born since 1985 and also known as Generation Y) are obsessed with being "always on, always connected" to the Internet and to their friends. Millennials are on track to grow by 1.3 billion to a total of 3 billion by the end of 2016.[1] This means they will account for 45 percent of world population by 2016.[2] Fifty percent of millennials perform research via the Web, and more than 90 percent purchase products via the Web.[3] In the U.S., today's 80 million millennials spend on average 11 hours per day digitally connected (53 hours per week).[4] These are staggering figures.

The one question that all millennials agree on is their mobile device of choice: the smartphone. Consider these sobering smartphone statistics:

- In 2014, 1.9 billion cell phones were sold worldwide,[5] of which 968 million were smartphones.[6]

- In 2014, mobile subscribers worldwide totaled 6.9 billion. The 2016 forecast calls for this figure to grow to 8.5 billion.[7]

- There are now more phones than toothbrushes worldwide.[8]

- U.S. smartphone penetration was 75 percent in 2014[9] and forecast to exceed 90 percent by the end of 2016.[10]

- Smartphone penetration worldwide is forecast to exceed 69 percent by 2017.[11]

- Americans spend on average more than 2.5 hours per day on their smartphones.[12]

- Mobile apps are exploding; there were 63 billion in 2012, 138 billion in 2014, and the forecast calls for 268 billion apps in 2017.[13]

- The mobile apps market is evidently in its early stages of growth and has plenty of room for expansion.

In 2012, for the first time ever, the worldwide mobile subscriber base witnessed an annual growth rate greater than that of the Internet. Research firm IDC projects that the number of worldwide mobile workers will reach 1.3 billion by the end of 2015. Most of these workers will be millennials who own a smartphone as well as multiple mobile devices, including tablets and/or some type of laptop. With the increase in the use of mobile devices and mobile apps, the market for mobility will explode. This raises additional questions:

- Can any organization survive in the future without a sound mobile strategy in place for its employees and its customers?
- Can an organization afford not to offer products/services via one or more apps?
- If the organization's two-way dialogue with its customers is not inclusive of the ability to communicate via mobile devices, will the organization be able to retain its customer base?

Millennials are important because they are the customers of the future and because they will fill most of the future jobs in sales, marketing, customer service, procurement, logistics, finance, and so on. Organizations need to understand the digital ecosystem in which millennials live and work, and help them to be successful within this ecosystem. This is why mobility is not just a millennial trend, but rather a business imperative.

## An Overview of Mobile Devices Used for Social CRM Applications

What is the most suitable business application that one can have on a mobile device? In 2013, this application was mobile CRM/sales force automation.[14] In 2018, I believe this application will be mobile Social CRM. There are four reasons driving the increasing adoption of mobile Social CRM.

### Reason 1: Mobile Devices

Two new mobile devices are stirring interest in mobile Social CRM: smartphones as pocket PCs, and tablets.

Smartphones are essentially pocket PCs on a mobile device. The three smartphone operating platforms to look out for in the next few years are as follows:

- Apple's iPhone OS
- Google's Android OS
- Microsoft's Mobile 8 OS

There is an intense battle going on between these smartphone products, with products such as the BlackBerry mobile OS on the way out.

Tablets are now the new mobile form factor. Most tablets on the marketplace today are based on the Google Android OS, although the new version of Windows 8 OS (Windows Blue) for tablets will intensify competition among tablet manufacturers. Renowned consultant Tim Bajarin, president of Creative Strategies, Inc., predicts that most tablets in the future will be sold with the screen size of 7 to 8 inches, which is what the Windows Blue OS is designed for.

In 2014, there were 216 million tablets sold worldwide. Tablets are increasingly replacing PCs and laptops; by the end of 2016, forecasts call for tablets outselling PCs/laptops for the first time.[15] Apple's tablet iPad led the way, but all PC vendors now offer tablets. Here's the reason why tablets will remain in vogue: They facilitate millennials to live easily within their "always on, always connected" ecosystem.

Tablets can now perform 80 to 90 percent of PC functionality. The 10 to 20 percent functionality that only a PC can perform includes heavy duties such as managing a media library, writing long documents, and performing sophisticated functions such as doing taxes. Given that tablets currently cannot completely replace the role of a PC, there will likely be an introduction of low-cost, touch-based clamshell PCs ($399–$599) that will usher in the era of good-enough computing for the masses. Midmarket PC sales ($699–$999) will dramatically drop, while the forecast calls for premium PC sales ($999–$1499) to hold up.

### Reason 2: Improved Networks

Improved networks and bandwidth are also helping to stir up interest and mobile Social CRM. There are now multinetworks/roaming with less latency, improved bandwidth, enhanced security, and affordability. Roaming is now considered the norm in today's market. The big push in the wireless market is toward 4G networks, as all carriers are rushing to get these faster networks to the market.

### Reason 3: Software Enhancements

There has been tremendous improvement in mobile apps and mobile software enhancements. Software vendors have not just rewritten their software to work on mobile devices but have also *optimized* their software for mobile devices. In addition to standard functions such as accounts, contacts, and tasks, mobile software now includes the following:

- Valuable built-in processes (for example, campaign management)
- Powerful dashboards
- Clean, ribbon-based interfaces
- In-context information
- Linkages to Social Media communities

### Reason 4: A Strong "What's in It for Me?" (WIIFM)

Mobile devices and the mobile software that runs on them help an organization to manage its business in the following ways:

- They allow for timely collaboration between field sales and executives (for example, customer response and updates; follow-up tracking; forecast, lead, and pipeline management).
- They reduce downtime, allowing employees to be productive all of the time (for example, in taxis, airports, and reception areas).
- They increase customer face time, allow for quicker responses to questions, and improve satisfaction.
- They provide access to real-time information at a person's fingertips (for example, account and order status, history look-ups, and available-to-promise inventory).
- They enable immediate action while the user is away from the office.

Millennials like their mobile devices because they serve multiple purposes:

- Mobile devices provide business tools, including phone, email, maps, and so on.

- Mobile devices offer productivity improvements (the user can easily access relevant customer and sales information, including what the customer bought, outstanding complaints, and so on).

- In addition to desired business apps, mobile devices provide access to lifecycle, entertainment, and personal productivity apps that can be used during downtime.

The WIIFM aspect has led to high user uptake of both mobile devices and the apps and software that run on these devices. Mobile devices have become the Swiss Army knife for field personnel. Here are typical mobile device user comments:

- "It's a part of my lifestyle."
- "It's portable."
- "It saves me time."
- "It's easy."
- "It's proactive."
- "It just works."
- "It keeps me organized."

BlackBerry conducted a study comparing mobile CRM to desktop/laptop CRM weekly usage. The study found that desktop/laptop users accessed their CRM application much less often during the week than mobile CRM users, and that desktop/laptop CRM users spent considerably more time on Sundays preparing their weekly reports than mobile CRM users, whose weekly reports were compiled throughout the week.[16]

# The Impact of Mobility on Social CRM

The biggest impact of mobility on Social CRM will be the ability for company personnel and customers to use their mobile devices to fulfill their Social CRM needs. Here are some examples:

- Sales reps remotely access the organization's customer profiles, including both transactional and sentiment insights gathered from Social Media communities, thereby helping the reps to sell smarter.

- Marketing personnel access and participate in Social Media communities directly from their mobile devices to secure insights from customers/prospects participating in those communities.
- Millennials use their mobile devices to receive special location-sensitive information.

Gartner estimates that in 2014, 1.9 billion smartphones were shipped worldwide[17] and 6.7 billion devices were connected to the Internet.[18] If Gartner's forecast is accurate, there will be 25 billion devices connected to the Internet by 2015 and 50 billion by 2020. This opens the door to entirely new ways to reach customers and prospects, resulting in large part from advancements in both mobile devices and mobile apps/software applications. New location and context push services will become the norm, whereby a customer or prospect is pushed a special promotion on their mobile device when they are in the vicinity of a specific location sensor or beacon (for example, a Marriott Rewards member might receive a $5 coupon when they are in or near a Marriott gift shop or a Starbucks located within the Marriott property).

In the next chapter, I discuss the growing importance of gamification and its impact on Social CRM.

# Endnotes

1. Pew Research, Creative Strategies & ISM Research.

2. Pew Research, Creative Strategies & ISM Research.

3. Pew Research, Creative Strategies & ISM Research.

4. Pew Research, Creative Strategies & ISM Research.

5. Gartner, "Gartner Says Worldwide Traditional PC, Tablet, Ultramobile and Mobile Phone Shipments on Pace to Grow 7.6 Percent in 2014," http://www.gartner.com/newsroom/id/2645115 (January 7, 2014).

6. Statista, "Number of smartphones sold to end users worldwide from 2007 to 2013," http://www.statista.com/statistics/263437/ global-smartphone-sales-to-end-users-since-2007/ (2013).

7. MobiForge, "Global mobile statistics 2014," http://mobiforge.com/ research-analysis/global-mobile-statistics-2014-part-a-mobile-subscribers-handset-market-share-mobile-operators (2014).

8. MobileMarketing, "More Mobile Phone Access than Toothbrushes, says Google," http://mobilemarketingmagazine.com/more-mobile-phone-access-toothbrushes-says-google/ (October 1, 2012).

9. MarketingLand, "Smartphone Penetration Likely to Be 75 Percent By Year End," http://marketingland.com/nearing-75-percent-smartphone-penetration-year-end-94903 (August 7, 2014).

10. MarketingLand, "Smartphones to Reach 90 Pct. In US, UK By 2016 — Forecast," http://marketingland.com/smartphones-reach-90-percent-us-uk-2016-forecast-82477 (May 2, 2014).

11. eMarketer, "Smartphone Users Worldwide Will Total 1.75 Billion in 2014," http://www.emarketer.com/Article/Smartphone-Users-Worldwide-Will-Total-175-Billion-2014/1010536 (January 16, 2014).

12. BGR, "Horrifying chart reveals how much time we spend staring at screens each day," http://bgr.com/2014/05/29/smartphone-computer-usage-study-chart/ (May 29, 2014).

13. Gartner, "Gartner Says Mobile App Stores Will See Annual Downloads Reach 102 Billion in 2013," http://www.gartner.com/newsroom/id/2592315 (September 19, 2013).

14. CRMSearch.com, "Sizing Up the CRM Software Market," http://www.crmsearch.com/crm-market.php (2013).

15. Gartner, "Gartner Says Tablet Sales Continue to Be Slow in 2015," http://www.gartner.com/newsroom/id/2954317 (January 5, 2015).

16. BlackBerry Private Conference Presentation Deck.

17. Gartner, "Gartner Says Worldwide Traditional PC, Tablet, Ultramobile and Mobile Phone Shipments on Pace to Grow 7.6 Percent in 2014," http://www.gartner.com/newsroom/id/2645115 (January 7, 2014).

18. Mediapost, "Brands Need Integrated Campaigns to Reach Connected Consumers," http://www.mediapost.com/publications/article/180556/brands-need-integrated-campaigns-to-reach-connecte.html (August 9, 2012).

# 21

## The Impact of Gamification on Social CRM

*Gamification* is defined as the use of applying game-like elements to non-game environments to influence behavior and the integration of game mechanics into a website, Social Media community, campaign, or application to drive engagement. Gamification allows an organization to benefit from the adoption of psychology techniques to motivate people to perform certain actions.

## Examples of Gamification in Business Situations

The advantages of applying gamification techniques to multiple business situations for an organization are many. To demonstrate the benefits of adopting gamification techniques, here are three outstanding examples of employing gamification for different business situations.

### Motivate Sales Reps to Use Social CRM Applications

Organizations that use the Salesforce.com Social CRM application have an option to purchase gamification vendor Bunchball's add-on module to help drive increased use of the application. Here are two example of how this works:

- Each time a rep completes a trip report, updates an address, or leverages social insight from a customer profile located in Salesforce.com, the user receives points in the adjacent Bunchball game console. The user then has the opportunity to redeem these points for merchandise or gift cards.

- The gamification application can create leaderboards to show how all sales reps are doing against each other in terms of sales, new leads, completed calls, and so on, thereby encouraging friendly competition among the reps.

## Increased Social Media Community Participation

Applying gamification techniques such as rewards and recognition to a Social Media community helps secure increased engagement by employees, customers, and partners. Community members get more points or higher recognition as they participate more in the community. Many Social Media platform vendors, including Jive, Lithium, and Mzinga, now offer a gamification component or plug-in to their platform.

Coca-Cola is a good example of a company that has turned to gamification to beef up its current Social Media efforts (My Coke Rewards at www.mycokerewards.com). Prior to revamping its site by adding a gamification component, the company concluded the following:[1]

> "The landscape of loyalty is also changing—Social Media, loyalty and Gamification are no longer independent. Coke is trying to leverage this evolution in the loyalty space by making the new My Coke Rewards experience inherently social and gamified. However, the traditional My Coke Rewards program does not have a mechanism to engage and reward those who want to socially engage with us. Our current, one-size-fits-all approach to loyalty doesn't work for everyone. So the new program will enable us to expand our reach by interacting with and rewarding members in new ways and at different levels."

## Lower Contact Center Agent Turnover

In general, contact centers are staffed with agents in low-paying positions who often must deal with unhappy customers in stressful situations. This leads to unhappiness at work and poor servicing of customers. It also leads to high turnover rates in the contact center—often in excess of 20 percent per year in many centers.

Gamification introduces fun into contact center agents' work. Agents earn points, for example, by hitting performance goals (for example, logging each call), earning training certifications, and interacting with others in the internal gamification community. Agents can apply for certain opportunities, choice of shifts, and so on. Agents can also earn badges to signify accomplished training and performance goals. Profile pages and leaderboards show agents where they stand. All this leads to friendly competition among contact center agents, which generates a win-win situation whereby agent satisfaction increases, they treat customers better, customer satisfaction goes up, and so on. Key contact center gamification applications include PlayVox and Verint.

LiveOps is a good example of an organization that has successfully applied gamification to its contact center for training, service, and sales. Headquartered in the heart of Silicon Valley, LiveOps is in the Cloud contact center space. It has more than 20,000 distributed contact center agents and has to onboard, train, and motivate these agents. LiveOps uses a gamification application called My Work Community, whereby agents can do the following:

- Earn points by hitting performance goals, completing certifications, and interacting with the community
- Apply for certain opportunities, choice of shift, and so on
- Receive badges that signify accomplished training and performance goals
- See where they stand from profile pages and leaderboards

The results to date for this gamification application have been quite impressive:[2]

- 80 percent of agents opted in to the gamification program, with 75 percent of them returning on a biweekly basis.
- 72 percent of agents completed certifications that weren't required, motivated only by gamification mechanics (volunteer learning).
- The onboarding process for a new client decreased from four weeks of classroom training to 14 hours.
- Service levels improved by about 10 percent.
- Average time to handle a customer inquiry decreased by almost 15 percent.
- Sales performance improved eight to 12 percent.

### *Deepen Customer Engagement*

ISM is working with a global hotel chain to help create an online game application that encourages rewards members to spend their rewards points. By spending their rewards points, these members have the opportunity to visit global properties where members receive very meaningful promotions to stay at these properties in the future. This game application serves two purposes: It helps members learn more about the chain's properties and provides members with meaningful discounts, and it helps the hotel to lower the growing number of redeemable rewards points that it must honor in the future.

# Game On!

Gamification applications are receiving a lot of attention at this time, and I am certain they will continue to grow significantly in the future. In 2010, there were 500 results for Google searches for *gamification.* Today there are 1,950 million results. In 2013, businesses spent $421 million on gamification applications. That figure is estimated to reach $5.5 billion in 2018.[3] Gartner predicts that by the end of 2015, gamification service for consumer-goods marketing and consumer retention will be as important as the effect of Facebook, eBay, and Amazon. Gartner also predicts that by the end of 2015, one half of Fortune 500 companies will have at least one gamification application up and running.[4]

Gamification is receiving such attention because it is capable of delivering meaningful business results:

- **Engagement**
  - Increase in Social Media community participation (for example, page views, user-generated content, time spent on site, and other)
  - Customer service agent retention
  - Friendly competition among sales personnel
- **Loyalty**
  - Increase in referrals
  - Increase in repeat visits
  - Increase in social sharing

- **Sales Impact**
  - Over 4 percent higher revenue growth in companies that use gamification (Aberdeen Group)
  - Increase in add-to-cart figures
  - Increase in conversions

# Deployment Options

There are various methods of deploying gamification applications. I cover three common ways to deploy gamification within an organizational environment in this section.

### *Using a Purpose-Built Gamification Custom App*

A good example is EpicMix, a gamification app for skiing developed by Vail Resorts Management Company and available to all skiers using Vail Resort mountains. The app tracks the lifts and ski trails that skiers are actively participating in each time they are on the slopes. For example, a skier who goes ten times on the same ski lift will obtain a Monogamous badge; a skier who skies normally in subzero weather will obtain a Polar badge. More than 100,000 skiers have signed up for the EpicMix custom app, including my ski buddies and I. We love this app because it makes skiing more fun, and we enjoy the friendly competition.

### *Building on Top of a Gamification Platform*

Badgeville, LevelUp, and Foursquare are good examples of this deployment option. Foursquare is a location-based Social Media community for mobile devices. Using a mobile website, text messaging, or a device-specific application, Foursquare users can select from a list of automatically generated, nearby venues that participate in the Foursquare community to learn more about each venue's products/services. Foursquare's application automatically matches location information based on GPS hardware in the user's mobile device and the network location of the participating vendor. Each time users post the writing of "Tips" (short messages or reviews concerning a venue), they are awarded points towards an "Expertise" in a particular location (for example, neighborhood) or category (for example, French restaurants). Expertise points are also awarded based on the quality of each tip (for example, number of views, saves, and "likes" received from other users).

Foursquare also allows users to "follow" their favorite organizations and receive special discounts from participating stores they are loyal to.

### Via a Gamification Service

Samsung Nation is an example of a gamification service deployment. Samsung Nation offers a social loyalty program where participants earn badges, move up in the ranks, and have fun discovering everything that Samsung.com has to offer. Users unlock badges and "level up" just by visiting, reviewing products, watching videos, participating in user-generated Q&As, and more. They also can see what others are doing in real time, and even uncover a few surprises along the way.

## The Impact of Gamification on Social CRM

Gamification is all about organizations applying social technology to time-tested, motivational methods. Millennials love to play games—they grew up playing them. Gamification within a business setting can help motivate millennial employees and customers to perform certain activities within their Social CRM system. Here is a list of exemplary ways that gamification impacts Social CRM:

- To motivate sales reps. (For example, each time a sales rep uploads a new lead from a Social Media community, the rep receives ten points and moves up in the leaderboard rankings. If the rep closes a $50,000 deal, the rep gets 1,000 points and receives the coveted Super Salesperson badge.)
- To encourage employees to review the latest information about the customer located with a customer profile to ensure that they are in the know when dealing with that customer.
- To encourage employees to continue to improve the organization's Social Media monitoring and filtering to ensure a steady stream of social insight information coming into the organization and into individual customer profiles.
- To encourage customers and partners to participate in the organization's internal and external Social Media communities so that they can earn points, badges, and other rewards as they participate.

- To better service customers because the contact center agent is a happy agent, in part resulting from being able to benefit from the gamification features within the Social CRM system.
- To improve marketing campaigns by providing marketers with points, badges, and other relevant rewards for tracking marketing campaigns and taking steps to improve these campaigns.

All Social CRM functions can be gamified to help drive enhanced utilization of those functions. This is why both Social Media platform vendors and Social CRM software vendors are adding more and more gamification functionality to their software (for example, awards, iconic badges, point systems, progress bars, and competitive rankings). These vendors aim to help organizations motivate their Social CRM system users to better leverage the Social CRM application in their day-to-day sales, marketing, and customer service activities. For all the reasons noted in this chapter and in the prior chapter on mobility, I am a big believer in gamification. Now is the time for organizations to jump onto the gamification bandwagon and begin to leverage its value-add in their Social CRM efforts.

In the next chapter, I discuss the business value of Big Data analytics and insight, and its impact on the Social CRM marketplace.

## Endnotes

1. COLLOQUY, "Q&A: Coke Refreshes Loyalty Program," https://www.colloquy.com/loyalty-strategies/q-a-coke-refreshes-loyalty-program/ (November 25, 2013).

2. Bunchball LiveOps Success Story, "How LiveOps reduced onboarding time for call center agents from weeks to hours," http://www.bunchball.com/customers/liveops (August 2014).

3. Marketsandmarkets, "Gamification Market worth $5.5 Billion By 2018," http://www.marketsandmarkets.com/PressReleases/gamification.asp (June 2013).

4. Gartner, "Gartner Says By 2015, More Than 50 Percent of Organizations That Manage Innovation Processes Will Gamify Those Processes," http://www.gartner.com/newsroom/id/1629214 (April 12, 2011).

# 22

## The Impact of Big Data Analytics and Insight on Social CRM

Big Data refers to data-driven, tactical decision-making derived from large data volumes coming from a variety of sources (transactional, Social Media, mobile devices, electronic transactions, and so on).

Big Data's growth over the past few years has been explosive. In 2013, businesses spent over $18 billion on Big Data services. By 2017, this figure is estimated to reach over $50 billion, which is almost a three-fold increase in four years.[1] This impressive growth is being driven in large part by decreasing costs for both data storage and data analytic tools, and a new business model for generating and consuming data. Regarding the latter, under the old model a few influential third-party data aggregators such as Experian and Acxiom gathered financial, demographic, behavior, and lifestyle data and then sold this data to organizations for their internal consumption. Around 2005, the model for data collection changed: Organizations began to generate, collect, and analyze their own customer data and then purchased "data overlays" from third-party data integrators, whereby

- the organization provides its customer data to the data aggregator,
- the data aggregator overlays this customer data with additional demographic, behavioral, and lifestyle data about each customer, and
- the data aggregator provides the data-rich customer file back to the organization for analysis, and ultimately customer engagement purposes

This new model puts the power of data analytics and insight back into the hands of the organization. The impact? More and more data is being generated, collected, and analyzed, as evidenced by these sobering statistics:

- Walmart handles one million transactions per hour.[2]
- Google processes 24 petabytes of data per day.[3]
- AT&T transfers 30 petabytes of data per day.[4]
- Over one hundred billion emails are sent per day.[5]
- Every hour, Internet traffic consumes data equal to seven million DVDs.[6]
- Google's Eric Schmidt claims that every two days now we create as much information as we did from the dawn of civilization up until 2003.[7]
- By 2020, one third of all data will be stored/passed through the Cloud, and 35 zetabytes of data will have been created.[8]

## Applying Big Data Successfully within the Business Environment

Let's briefly examine how a few organizations are putting Big Data analysis and insight to work:

- **The American Automobile Association** has been providing services to its members for more than 100 years. Although a majority of the more than 50 million members often think of AAA as the tow company, AAA offers many additional valuable services, including insurance for vehicles, home, life and health, commercial, and travel. To drive up insurance revenues, AAA clubs have turned to Big Data to help determine which members to offer insurance to, which insurance products to offer, and the best time to approach a member with AAA insurance offerings.
- **State Farm Insurance** automobile division determined some time ago that to accurately assess the risk associated with insuring an individual's car, it needed more than the traditional demographic variables—age, sex, location of the vehicle, and so on. This is why the company recently teamed up with a third party to offer the Drive Safe & Save In-Drive program, which promises that "the

safer you drive, the more you save on your State Farm auto insurance." By installing inside a customer's car a technology device that monitors the customer's driving behavior, State Farm is able to collect additional valuable information to assess how often the customer drives the car, the distance typically driven, how often the customer brakes heavily, and so on. The In-Drive program data complements existing demographic data and allows State Farm to build Big Data models that analyze this data so that in the near future, State Farm can offer the right insurance product at the right price to each user based on the unique driving characteristics and needs of that user.

- **Sysco** (the organization that distributes food to many of the more than one million foodservice locations—called *operators*—in the United States) was one of the earliest users of Big Data. By creating sophisticated data models, Sysco was able to analyze local purchase patterns to be able to recommend to operators exactly what products they should be purchasing to optimize business sales. This has created a valuable collaboration between Sysco and the operators, to the envy of most of the food manufacturers that would like, but do not have, this kind of partnership with operators.

- **Pacific Life** wanted to sell additional annuities, life insurance, and mutual funds through its Financial Advisor (FA) network. To do this, it leveraged Big Data modeling tools to determine who were the best Financial Advisors (FAs), inclusive of identifying the high-potential FAs and why. With this knowledge in hand, Pacific Life created a game plan to improve FA sales performance via an effective cross/upsell program, as well as to improve operational efficiency by targeting the best FAs for identified products. A byproduct of this Big Data modeling was a better understanding of when FAs churn and what to do to increase the retention of targeted FAs.

# The Components of Effective, Data-Driven Decision-Making

Although there is no shortage of Big Data analytics opportunities within an organization, succeeding at implementing Big Data analytics is no slam-dunk. The following seven requirements need to be in place:

- **Big Data analytics strategy and goals**—Why is the organization embarking on a Big Data analytics effort? What are the goals? What problems need to be fixed? The most popular analytics applications include customer segment profiling, customer engagement activities, customer journey mapping, customer potential (for example, product association, including "basket analysis," propensity to purchase, and next-best-offer/next-best-action), customer acquisition/retention/churn, customer lifetime value, customer channel optimization, and marketing campaign optimization.

- **Quality data**—Does the organization have the necessary data in place to perform the required analysis and is the data quality where it needs to be? Take an inventory of available customer data and its quality. Where possible, make corrections to alleviate data quality issues. Tapping into the large selection of valuable customer and industry data sources, including third-party data sets and overlays (that is, demographics, behavioral, lifestyle, and technographics), facilitates this. Creativity in data acquisition is paramount.

- **Meaningful data analysis**—Performing meaningful data analysis cannot be left to either the business or the IT side of the organization. It requires a collaborative effort between both sides. On the one hand, the business side needs to fulfill the role of the "creative" marketer to determine how to secure more real-time data coming from brand-loyal customers who are often sensitive to privacy issues. On the other hand, the IT side needs to fill the role of the "technical" marketer to harness more real-time data coming from external sources, leverage the new data tools, and deliver meaningful business insights coming from the data analysis. The focus should be on the analysis and resulting business insights, not the manipulation of the data. If required skill sets do not currently exist within the organization, consider engaging external SMEs.

- **Well-trained managers/executives**—I continue to be amazed by how few executives have grabbed the data-analytics bull by the horns and put it to use. Perhaps this is an issue of training managers and executives on how to use data-driven insights to make better business decisions. In best-in-class organizations, data-driven decision-making is a core value. Make data insights actionable.

- **Meaningful measurement and monitoring**—Set metrics at the outset and measure these metrics carefully throughout the data-analytics initiative. This is important for creating baselines and benchmarks to be applied as the organization's data-analytics efforts expand.

- **Implementation of a benchmarking program**—Data-driven decision-making is not a one-off event. With several of ISM's customers, we are into second-, third-, or even fourth-generation data models that use both quantitative (transactional) and qualitative (from customer interviews and surveys) data to provide deeper insights. Start with low-volume data-analytics trials. Document what worked and what did not. Continue to benchmark results so that the organization realizes incremental gains.

- **Tight integration with Social CRM efforts**—I discuss this requirement in the following paragraph.

# The Impact of Big Data on Social CRM

Big Data analytics and insight are already having a meaningful impact on the way organizations manage their customer relationships and customer engagements. Best-in-class organizations have already concluded that to be successful, Big Data must be tightly integrated into their Social CRM application. This includes, for example, the following tasks:

- Integrating data insights into customer profiles contained within Social CRM applications. (For example, which products should be offered to which customers? Which customers and prospects should sales reps call on? Which next-best-offer should be made via the contact center or via the Web? What is the next step in the customer journey?)

- Identifying new and creative market segments for use in Social CRM marketing programs.

- Providing guidance on optimizing marketing campaigns across all relevant channels that get created and launched from within the Social CRM application.

- Determining the best topics for a Social Media community to drive high customer engagement and social insights that will be integrated in the Social CRM application.

Here's the good news: More and more Social CRM systems are offering meaningful data-analytics tools either within their software or via integration with external data-analytics tools to help organizations turn data insights into sales, marketing, and customer service excellence. Key Social CRM vendors such as Oracle, Salesforce.com, and SAP have begun to invest heavily in Big Data tools.

Similar to gamification, Big Data is in its infancy; its impact has yet to be truly felt. Over the next five to ten years, Big Data analytics and insight tools—along with their integration into Social CRM—will take organizations to the next level of creating and sustaining meaningful two-way dialogues with their customers, and will play a meaningful role in enhancing customer satisfaction, loyalty, and advocacy.

In the next chapter, I discuss the growing importance of channel optimization and its impact on Social CRM.

# Endnotes

1. Wikibon, "Big Data Vendor Revenue and Market Forecast 2013-2017," http://wikibon.org/wiki/v/Big_Data_Vendor_Revenue_and_Market_Forecast_2013-2017 (February 12, 2014).

2. SAS, "Big Data Meets Big Data Analytics," http://www.sas.com/resources/whitepaper/wp_46345.pdf (2012).

3. MIT Sloan Management Review, "How Big Data is Different," http://sloanreview.mit.edu/article/how-big-data-is-different/ (July 30, 2012).

4. Sourcelink, "The 5Ws and 1H of Big Data," http://www.sourcelink.com/blog/guest-author-series/2012/08/18/the-5ws-and-1h-of-big-data-%28part-2-of-2%29 (August 18, 2012).

5. THE RADICATI GROUP, INC, "Email Statistics Report, 2013-2017," http://www.radicati.com/wp/wp-content/uploads/2013/04/Email-Statistics-Report-2013-2017-Executive-Summary.pdf (April 2013).

6. Atelier, "Data and the Internet Take a Lot of Space In the Real World," http://www.atelier.net/en/trends/articles/data-and-internet-take-lot-space-real-world (January 5, 2012).

7. TechCrunch, "Eric Schmidt: Every 2 Days We Create As Much Information As We Did Up To 2003," http://techcrunch.com/2010/08/04/schmidt-data/ (August 4, 2010).

8. AnalyticsWeek, "Factoid to Give Big-Data a Perspective," http://analyticsweek.com/factoid-give-big-data-perspective/ (September 30, 2013).

# 23

## The Impact of Channel Optimization on Social CRM

All organizations at one time or another have dealt with happy and unhappy customers, profitable and unprofitable customers, and high- and low-maintenance customers. What if an organization had a magic wand that optimized the channel(s) that customers use so that each customer gets to use the preferred channel(s) while the organization maximizes the profitability of each customer by encouraging each to use the optimal channel(s), based on the organization's cost-to-serve the customer? Sound enticing? I hope so, because beyond doubt channel optimization is the most important area that impacts an organization's profitability. Channel optimization also meaningfully impacts the way that an organization uses its Social CRM tools to engage with its customers.

As shown in Figure 23.1, there are two parts to channel optimization. The first part deals with achieving a balance between fulfilling each customer's desired channel preferences and achieving the organization's desire to secure the lowest cost-to-serve channel option for each customer.

Organizations will have to take the necessary steps to learn which channel(s) their customers prefer to use to engage with the organization (for example, email, face-to-face meetings, telephone calls with contact center personnel, direct mail, dialogue on public or private Social Media channels, in-store face-to-face discussions, mobile apps, and a website/ecommerce portal). To secure this information, organizations need to (1) perform analysis of their customers' channel preferences today (determined by their current purchase behavior with the organization) and (2) undertake market research to determine each customer's future channel preferences.

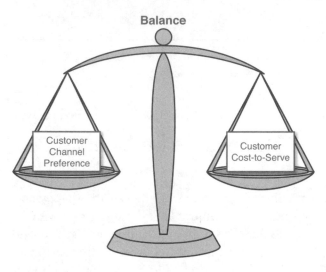

**Figure 23.1** Channel optimization

Organizations need to ask these two questions regarding cost-to-serve: Does the organization know how much it costs to serve each customer via the customer's preferred channel(s), and is the organization making or losing money serving customers via their preferred channel(s)? Determining cost-to-serve requires careful analysis of all relevant channel financials for existing and planned channels. This can be a challenging exercise because many organizations do not track their metrics; however, channel optimization cannot be achieved without this input.

The challenge is to find the right balance between delivering the desired customer channel preferences and driving customers to the lowest cost-to-serve channel acceptable to them. No easy task, and complicated further by a number of additional challenges:

- **Should an organization use a single or multichannel strategy?** Many customers and organizations work in a few channels today, but this will not be true in the future. All organizations wishing to survive will have to put into place a multichannel strategy in which customers or prospects begin their customer journey in one channel (for example, via the Web), then move to another channel (for example, the contact center) to get answers to questions they did not find in the first channel, and, finally, move to a third channel (for example, your retail store) to make a purchase.

- **Will a customer's channel preference(s) change?** Think about how customers' preferences have changed in the book, music, travel, and shopping industries over the past decade. If customer preferences begin to change within your industry, how will this impact your organization's ability to serve these customers?

- **What is the ease of moving customers to the other channel?** I worked with a global footwear and apparel company that sought to put into place a lowest cost-to-serve strategy. The company encouraged certain customer segments to move from full service to digital channels to accomplish this. The strategy hit resistance because customers were not ready for the change and needed considerably more training than initially anticipated.

- **What are the channel costs—learning curve implications?** Certain channels may seem expensive to work in today, but as these channels are used more, costs will come down due to the learning curve (for example, think about the cost to start up a Social Media community five years ago and how much that cost has decreased in price today).

The second part of channel optimization deals with optimizing each selected channel through the use of integrated processes and technology (see Figure 23.2).

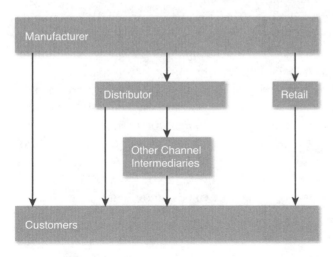

**Figure 23.2** Option channels

I recently performed primary research on ten best-in-class global organizations that have successfully integrated distribution channels. They include Armstrong, Caterpillar, DuPont, Johnson Controls, Kraft Foods, Microsoft, Monsanto, Steelcase, Sysco, and Volvo Construction Equipment. Most of these companies have focused on putting into place business processes supported by Social CRM technology in sales pipeline/opportunity management, partner relationship management, marketing initiatives, and/or Social Media community building. Each company had meaningful challenges when putting into place the right business processes (for example, sales pipeline management) and then configuring the Social CRM software to drive efficiency into these processes. Yet those companies that *put the right processes and technology* into place with their distributors are running away from the pack.

It is challenging to reach an agreement on common core business processes with channel partners, which are all typically independent organizations. Take the sales pipeline management process as an example. Almost all organizations already have some kind of sales pipeline management in place, so if a manufacturer asks distribution channel partners to all use the same sales pipeline management process, one or more of the organizations likely will either have to modify its own sales pipeline process or have to enter sales pipeline information twice—once into the company sales pipeline system and a second time into the common sales pipeline management system.

Both options present challenges, but my research with best-in-class organizations overwhelmingly confirms that once a core business process such as sales pipeline management has been aligned with distribution-channel partners, and technology has been put into place to drive efficiency into the core business process, tremendous benefits are realized by all distribution channel partners. These benefits result from the speedier flow of information between channel partners, resulting in, for example, the ability to pass sales leads more efficiently, to easily track sales leads, to look into inventory levels in real time, to easily exchange needed information and reports, and overall to be in a position to better service channel partners because everyone is on the same page.

# Summary of Key Channel Optimization Challenges

An organization's channel optimization effort will inevitably encounter problems. Based on my many years of experience, here is a broader summary of key organizational channel optimization challenges:

## New and More Channels, Each with Its Own Cost Structure

How will distribution channels change in the future? Will the Social Media channel become increasingly important? How will an organization's contact centers be impacted by new web-based services? What will be the cost to support additional channels, and will the ROI justify these costs? For example, in the case of AAA, will it make sense to continue to support the seven channels (emergency road service personnel, branch offices, contact centers, direct mail, Web, mobile, and Social Media) that it works in?

## Changing Customer Channel Preferences

Look at what happened to music stores, travel agencies, and bookstores. Once customers change their preference to an alternative channel from the one they customarily use, how will that impact the organization's channel-optimization strategy?

## The Need for Seamless Integration across Multichannels

Today's customers increasingly expect an organization to work with the customer in a multichannel environment. The onus is on the organization to carry relevant information from one channel to the next as the customer utilizes multiple channels (for example, the customer starts the buying process via the Web, calls the contact center for clarification of some points, and purchases the product in a local branch office). Integration across multichannels is expensive and technologically challenging, and needs to be carefully thought out by the organization and its participating distribution-channel partners.

### Performing Ongoing Data Analytics Regarding Channel Optimization

To achieve channel optimization, it is important that organizations leverage the latest data-analytics tools to monitor customer-channel preferences, channel usage by segment, and cost-to-serve within each channel.

### Getting the Preference-Versus-Cost Balance Right

How does the organization rectify the situation where a low-profit customer prefers to use the highest cost-to-serve channel? Getting this balance right is not always easy.

### Securing Customer Adoption of Lowest Cost-to-Serve Channels

I have been working with global, best-in-class organizations on channel-optimization strategies for three decades. I will never forget the time that ISM agreed on the go-to-market channel optimization strategy for a global footwear and apparel company, but failed to appreciate how difficult it would be to entice customers to move to the lowest cost-to-serve channels.

### Achieving Technology Integration across Channels

Even when customers or distribution-channel partners agree to use a common process, it can be very challenging to technically integrate systems to support the agreed-on common process.

Any organization wishing to exist in ten years will have to execute a sound channel-optimization strategy. That strategy must answer at least these two questions: Is the organization optimizing channel-partner integration, the channels that their customers use, or both? And how is the organization accommodating multichannel optimization? If the organization has good answers to these two questions, here's the bonus question: Where does the emerging Internet of Things (IOT) channel (discuss in the next chapter) fit into the organization's channel-optimization strategy?

# The Impact of Channel Optimization on Social CRM

Channel optimization impacts the very core of Social CRM—namely, which channels the organization will engage in with its customers and partners. If the organization does not agree on a sound channel-optimization strategy, even the best Social CRM system will be unable to rectify this deficiency. But if the organization does agree on a sound channel optimization strategy, it then needs to integrate the output of this strategy into the Social CRM system. The output includes, for example, placing relevant channel preference/lowest cost-to-serve information about a customer directly into one of the customer profile petals for use by the organization and channel partners in the customer-engagement process.

Given the tremendous growth of the Social Media channel and its role in generating social insight used by the Social CRM system, it is also imperative that the Social Media channel be tightly integrated into the organization's channel-optimization strategy.

The next chapter focuses on the Internet of Things, which will have a major impact on Social CRM and has the potential to revolutionize in the near future the way business is conducted globally.

# 24

## The Impact of the Internet of Things on Social CRM

Most (if not all) of an organization's products and services will be connected to the Internet in the future. These connections form a key part of the Internet of Everything (IOE) and its more important counterpart, the Internet of Things (IOT). Let's start with some definitions.

## Internet of Everything

The *Internet of Everything (IOE)* is a back-office term and vision coined by Cisco, the worldwide leader in networking. The IOE transforms how people connect, communicate, and collaborate. It can be defined as a global system of interconnected computer networks, sensors, actuators, and devices, all using the Internet protocol. It holds so much potential to change people's lives that it is often referred to as the Internet's next generation.

Cisco predicts that there will be 25 billion devices connected to the Internet by the end of 2015 and 50 billion devices connected by 2020, or on average seven connected devices for each person on Earth.[1] This remarkable prediction has far-reaching consequences, including a huge expansion in the generation, analysis, and use of Big Data; the availability of a new distribution channel and its integration in an organization's channel-optimization strategy; and enhancements to how organizations engage with their customers and prospects.

Three different types of Internet connectivity support the 50 billion-device prediction:

- **Machine-to-machine (for example, robots and sensors)—** Here, IOE sensors located on a machine (or product) are either sensing or actuating something, and subsequently instructing another machine to perform a resulting action.

- **Machine-to-people (for example, wearable and home security)**—Here, IOE sensors on a machine (or product) are communicating relevant information to a person, prompting this person to take a resulting action.

- **People-to-people (for example, social networks)**—As noted in Chapter 1, "Social CRM: The Intersection of Social Media and CRM," there currently are 1.7 billion people connecting to Social Media communities. These people use the Internet protocol via their mobile devices, PCs, and tablets.

The IOE is supported by a new technical architecture called Internet protocol version 6 (IPv6). IPv6 includes a huge increase in Internet address space that allows for an Internet address for every atom on the surface of the earth, with still enough addresses left to do another 100-plus earths. In other words, organizations and its customers could easily assign an Internet address to every *thing* on the planet.

# The Internet of Things

Closely related to the IOE is the *Internet of Things (IOT)*, which can be defined as "a scenario in which objects, animals, or people are provided with unique identifiers and the ability to transfer data over a network without requiring human-to-human or human-to-computer interaction."[2] Figure 24.1 helps illustrate this definition.

In the IOT, services such as App Store, Dropbox, Kindle, and Skype, and so on connect to the Cloud, which provides computer services over the Internet. Each of these services in turn connects to items/devices such as laptops, cars, televisions, refrigerators, medical devices, and more, so that data can be passed between them and the Cloud. Devices that have a built-in, machine-to-machine communication capabilities are referred to as *smart devices* (for example, smart label, smart meter, and smart grid sensor). Let's further explore some of the items/devices that comprise the IOT.

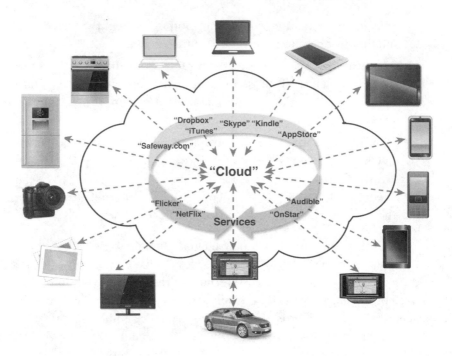

**Figure 24.1** The impact of the IOT

## Connected Home

The IOT connects different devices located in the home to the Cloud. Here are some of the more popular home devices on display at the 2014 Consumer Electronics Show:

- A digital door lock connected to the Cloud. When a cell phone with the proper code is placed in front of the digital door lock, the door lock opens. The lock can also be opened/closed from anywhere over the Internet.

- An Apple home-automation application connected to the Cloud. At night, users inform the application when they are going to sleep, which triggers the turning off of lights and the setting of other sleep time conditions (for example, the thermostat lowers the temperature). When people wake up, they indicate this via their iPhone, and all home settings automatically adjust back to daytime conditions.

- Animal collars that enable owners to track their animals regardless of where they may roam.

- Internet-connected crockpots, ovens, and refrigerators. At present, these devices can be turned on and off and the temperature can be adjusted via the Internet. In the future, I envisage that these devices will also know when the chicken is cooked and inform the homeowner that dinner is ready to be served.

## Connected Wearables

Various connected wearables are available in the marketplace today, including the following:

- Google Glass
- Smart-gear
- Nike Fuel

Google Glass is perhaps the most prominent connected wearable in the current marketplace. As an illustration of the potential benefits of connected wearable devices, Google Glass can take pictures and record video when the wearer has the device on. These recordings and related information subsequently are exported to a database for the type of Big Data analysis discussed in Chapter 22, "The Impact of Big Data Analytics and Insight on Social CRM." Google is also working on additional applications for the Google Glass device.

Connected wearables are an intermediate step toward the future. An even greater impact will be felt in society as connected wearable sensors are embedded into people's clothes for multiple uses. For example, children's clothing will soon have sensors to record a child's motions and can provide alerts to the parent concerning a child's location or activities.

## Connected Health

There was a lot of buzz at the 2014 Consumer Electronics Show about health-related IOT applications. Vendors displayed a wearable sensor that indicates the wearer's level of insulin, which can send this information to an iPhone, as well as a connected toothbrush that monitors how often users brush their teeth.

In the future, I envision that pillboxes will have sensors to inform patients that they forgot to take their medicine. I also envision (similar to the State Farm In-Drive program described in Chapter 22) that patients will wear health-related monitoring devices that connect to a patient's healthcare organization's database. The healthcare organization will perform analysis on a member's daily activities and create individual incentives to stay healthy. Such incentives will hopefully provide a boost for each employee to conduct healthy habits, and may also lead to decreased healthcare costs based on each person's health profile.

## Connecting Merchants with Customers

Here are two significant IOT technologies impacting merchant-customer relationships:

### Beacons

A *beacon* is a very small transmitting radio that sends relevant information to a desired location. Beacons utilize Bluetooth Low Energy technology, a wireless technology standard for exchanging data efficiently over short distances from fixed and mobile devices. A person in the proximity of a beacon or a person with a mobile app that communicates with the beacon will receive messages transmitted from that beacon. Here are a couple of examples of beacons in action:

- **Shopping at Macy's**—When a person walks into a Macy's store looking for blue jeans (assuming the shopper has already downloaded the Macy app on their smartphone), the beacon will notice that the person is in the blue jean aisle and transmit a special offer to the shopper via their smartphone for, say, a 40 percent discount for a particular brand of blue jeans if purchased within the next 30 minutes.

  Macy's beacon-generated data can then be analyzed over time to determine critical pieces of information for a business, such as where in a store the average consumer is spending the most time, what departments the consumer is spending the most money in, what coupons the consumer is using, and so on. Store planners can use this information to arrange items in the store to drive maximum customer interest and store sales.

- **Attending a San Francisco 49ers game at Levi's Stadium**—This marvelous new stadium has beacons located throughout the building. As game attendees that have downloaded the stadium app to their mobile device arrive at the stadium, they automatically receive instructions and a map showing where their seats are and how to get to them. During the football game, beacons will send time-sensitive discounts to attendees on their mobile devices (for example, an electronic coupon for a half-priced meal or a 30 percent discount on a 49ers' jersey that will be good for the next 30 minutes). The beacon application will even store data about the stadium meals that the attendee has eaten at prior games and tailor the electronic promotion to them.

### Wi-Fi Technology

More and more retailers are deploying Wi-Fi technology directly inside their stores. This already includes paying for merchandise electronically at the checkout counter. In the future, there will be many new IOT services and consumer offerings available via Wi-Fi, which is a cost effective way to conduct proximity-based communications with customers.

## Six Questions to Ask Regarding the Future of the Internet of Everything/Internet of Things

As with any new technology, plenty of questions need to be asked regarding the Internet of Everything/Internet of Things. Here are my top six questions and initial responses to each.

### Is There a Sustainable Driving Force Behind the IOE/IOT?

The demand for these technologies is driven by organizations' need for valuable customer, partner, and employee insights. The next two years will serve as a warm-up period in which people will be experimenting with IOE/IOT devices and applications. Some will take root and others will fall by the wayside. While B2C organizations will lead the charge during this period via connected home, connected wearables, and connected health devices, B2B organizations will also actively participate in such areas as deliveries, managing stock, inventory control, and customer analysis.

After this two-year period, during which time the bugs will get worked out, I predict that the IOE/IOT will take off. This era will be one of the most disruptive periods in modern history, as the IOE/IOT becomes a normal part of how customers manage their day-to-day activities in the home, office, and elsewhere.

## How to Cost-Justify Investing in the IOE/IOT?

As with all technology investments, a well-thought-out business case is the best way to justify investing in the IOE/IOT. Cost components in the business case include the following:

- The cost of the sensors and devices included within an item (refrigerator, medical device, and so on), or the cost of adding a sensor or device to an existing item
- The cost of creating a service in the Cloud to monitor these sensors and devices
- The cost of analyzing data coming from these sensors and devices

The revenue component of the business case results from looking at the lift in sales resulting from customers using these sensors and devices and comparing this to a control group that does not use these sensors and devices. Although not a perfect science, this approach is used by most of my customers to justify the ROI and breakeven point for a new technology (for example, the Front Runner Social Media community case study described in Chapter 3, "Social Media Pilot Case Study").

## How to Respond to the Growing Concerns around Data Privacy Issues?

This is a tough question to which there is no simple answer. Most organizations currently utilize the opt-in/opt-out approach to data privacy, as well as legal guidelines related to using customer data for marketing campaigns. For example, if beacon technology is used in a marketing campaign, consumers are required to download the organization's campaign app, turn the Bluetooth option on for location-based services, and grant permission to use the beacon-generated data for marketing purposes. Yet, because approaches and guidelines to data privacy are evolving, the IOE/IOT industry must actively contribute to this ongoing dialogue.

Typically, customers are willing to grant access to their private information if there are tangible benefits. If organizations can show their customers that there is a value in granting access to their private data, along with an explicit promise to not abuse the use of such data, then data privacy issues can often be met with mutual satisfaction on both sides. In essence, privacy is an organization/customer trust issue where trust gets built over time.

## What Are the Resulting Customer Service Challenges?

The resulting customer service challenges include the following:

- **New contact center support requirements**—I foresee the contact centers of the future offering support across most if not all channels, including telephone, Web, SMS messaging, Social Media, and IOT. These channels then feed into one dashboard that is located on the contact center rep's PC or other device.

- **Potential need for enhanced customer service**—Customers will have more questions and problems concerning IOE/IOT, and this will require enhanced customer service.

- **Role of mobility in customer service**—As mobile devices interact more with IOT devices/sensors, consumers will use more of their mobile devices to access customer service functions.

As the market grows, information flowing to and from sensors and devices will also grow, as will customer service requests—which may begin to overburden existing contact center capabilities. This is why I foresee organizations increasingly creating well-thought-out algorithms to receive IOE/IOT customer service requests and redirecting these requests to the right resources—likely to include more self-service functionality and tutorials—for an appropriate response.

## What Is the Impact on Big Data Analysis and Insight?

I discussed the need for business and IT personnel to collaborate on Big Data issues in Chapter 22. This holds equally true for data coming from the IOT sensors and devices: The organization's creative marketers must determine how to best leverage the real-time data coming from sensors and devices, while the technical marketers must harness real-time data coming from sensors and devices to deliver smarter decision-making. Together, they must answer the question, "Based on the data we are receiving from the Internet of Things sensors and devices, what products or services should we be offering, to whom and when?"

This implies a likely need for most organizations to enhance the data-analytics capacity required to assimilate the billions of sensors providing data and billions of devices connected to one another. It may also imply a need to secure additional data-analytics skills, either internally or via external SME.

## How to Address New People, Process, and Technology Issues?

When a new technology such as the IOE/IOT arrives on the scene, I find it helpful to ask, "What are the people, process, and technology issues that must be overcome to fully exploit this new technology?" Here are my current observations:

### People Issues
- Providing necessary training to corporate users (both business and IT) who are responsible for utilizing the IOE/IOT technology to achieve deeper business insights. Necessary time must be put aside to ensure that proper training takes place.
- Overcoming concerns around data privacy.

### Process Issues
- Readying the organization to systematically collect, process, and use data insight from the IOT sensors and devices.
- Determining the impact of the IOE/IOT on the organization's customer engagement activities, including, for example, new customer loyalty program opportunities.
- Enhancing technographic profiles to take into account how customers participate in the IOT and the resulting impact this has on achieving meaningful customer segmentation.
- Establishing privacy policies that allow customers to actively participate in the IOE/IOT.

### Technology Issues
- Addressing ongoing concerns regarding security of the IOE/IOT infrastructure. The small, embedded computers at the center of the IOT have minimal processing power or memory, so the security software on IOT applications tends to be elementary. There have been cases of hackers taking control of webcams, televisions, and even a refrigerator plugged into a computer network to send out spam.

- Closing the gap around the disparity of prevalent wireless standards that impacts the ability for sensors and devices to talk with each other.

- Closing infrastructural gaps between the sensors in the devices at the edge of the Internet and the data collection and analysis performed by the servers in the Cloud.

- Resolving middleware issues that impact the services connected to this Cloud. These issues include standards, interoperability, integration, and data management.

There are a number of other IOE/IOT issues, including product liability, intellectual property rights, and regulatory compliance. I can understand why a reader might conclude that the IOE/IOT is not ready for prime time. Keep in mind that when Internet technology arrived on the scene in the 1990s, critics pointed to its shortcomings in areas such as standardization, security, and lack of regulation, which would prevent the Internet from meaningfully impacting people's lives. Yet the value that people found in using the Internet was so great that businesses and governments cooperated to overcome these specified shortcomings and bring about a worldwide revolution whose impact we are only beginning to feel. I predict that over the next three to five years, IOE/IOT technology will undergo a similar degree of cooperation among businesses and governments to bring about a far-reaching transformation in the way organizations engage with their customers and partners.

## The Impact of the Internet of Things on Social CRM

The Internet of Things is in its infancy, so it is hard to accurately predict its impact on Social CRM. Yet, the more an organization knows about its customers' needs, desires, and behaviors, the better the organization can serve them. The IOT provides a tremendous opportunity to gain additional customer insights resulting from data coming from IOT sensors and devices. This new data will need to be monitored and filtered in a similar fashion to the way that Social Media community information is, and then exported into Social CRM systems for use in customer engagement activities. This includes the generation of new products and services tailored to newly identified customer segments.

In Part VII, "The Future of Social CRM," I have described six trends and my current thinking on the impact of these trends on Social CRM. Their impact on Social CRM will change as they and the Social CRM industry mature. The future looks promising!

Thank you for taking the time to read *The Definitive Guide to Social CRM*. I would be delighted to receive your comments or thoughts regarding the topics raised in this book. Also, if I, or my company, ISM, Inc., can be of service to you or your organization in the future, please do not hesitate to contact me (bgoldenberg@ismguide.com).

## Endnotes

1. Cisco, "The Internet of Things: How the Next Evolution of the Internet Is Changing Everything," http://www.cisco.com/web/about/ac79/docs/innov/IoT_IBSG_0411FINAL.pdf (April 2011).

2. WhatIs.com, "Internet of Things (IoT)," Internet of Things (IoT).

# Part VIII
Appendixes

# Social Media Policy Examples

The following are three excellent examples of exemplary organizational Social Media policies.

## Ford's Social Media Policies

Ford—usually considered an old-fashioned company—has one of the best Social Media policies. Its Social Media guidelines for engaging on the Social Web comprise the following core principles:

- *Honesty about who you are.*
- *Clarity that your opinions are your own.*
- *Respect and humility in all communications.*
- *Good judgment in sharing only public information—including financial data.*
- *Awareness that what you say is permanent.*

## Best Buy's Social Media Policies

Best Buy's Social Media policies are a good example of the consequences if an employee violates the policies:

*Be smart. Be respectful. Be human. Guidelines for functioning in an electronic world are the same as the values, ethics, and confidentiality policies employees are expected to live every day, whether you're Twittering, talking to customers, or chatting over the neighbor's fence. Remember, your responsibility to Best Buy doesn't end when you are off the clock. For that reason, this policy applies to both company sponsored Social Media and personal use.*

*Basically, if you find yourself wondering if you can talk about something you learned at work—don't. Follow Best Buy's policies and live the company's values and philosophies. They're there for a reason.*

*Just in case you are forgetful or ignore the guidelines, here's what could happen. You could:*

- *Get fired (and it's embarrassing to lose your job for something that's so easily avoided)*
- *Get Best Buy in legal trouble with customers or investors*
- *Cost us the ability to get and keep customers*

*Remember: protect the brand; protect yourself.*

## Greteman Group's Social Media Policies

Greteman Group, an advertising and consulting firm, is another good example of an organization leading a proactive, yet positive Social Media effort. Here are some key statements in the Greteman Group's Social Media policy:

*We are a plugged-in people, constantly bombarded by friend requests, photo tags, status updates, and links to videos of funny babies and pets. At Greteman Group, we not only embrace the media and technology that make these bombardments possible, we harness them for our clients. We also welcome the power of individuals to leverage and enhance their personal brands through these tools.*

*At the same time, we recognize the challenges of the increasing competition for our time and attention created by this barrage of messages. To address these challenges, we have created the following guidelines for team members' use of Social Media tools both in and out of the office.*

*Overall Philosophy:*

*While you are on company time, please refrain from online activities that don't bring value to the Greteman Group. Think of your personal time online in the same way you think of personal phone calls or emails.*

*Blogging:*

*Microsoft has a bone-simple blogging policy. Be smart. We ask the same of you. Please be smart in your online activities. They reflect on both you and the agency. The ability to publish things that may never go away and can be forwarded endlessly gives us pause, and we hope it does you, too.*

*We view personal websites and blogs as good things. We want you to avail yourselves of these media. We respect your online activity as a medium of self-expression. Please note, though, that confidentiality agreements prevent disclosure of all client and Greteman Group business.*

# B

## Leading Social Media Monitoring and Filtering Tools

The following are some of the top Social Media monitoring/filtering tools available:

- **Radian6**—Comprehensive coverage (150 million public sites); Social Media metrics and filtering into Salesforce.com; automated sentiment analysis; now owned by Salesforce.com.

- **Collective Intellect**—Real-time text mining and analytics; spam management; trend analysis; semantic search; now owned by Oracle.

- **Scout Labs**—Auto-determining sentiment of Social Media content; Social Media community monitoring, filtering, and analysis of customer conversations; now owned by Lithium Technologies.

- **Cisco SocialMiner**—Social Media community monitoring, queuing, and workflow to organize/filter/route relevant community customer posts.

- **Attensity**—Monitors social conversations (more than 75 million online sources); categorizes Social Media community content; routing of Social Media community content to an integrated Social CRM system (Salesforce.com, SAP, and Oracle-Siebel).

- **Simplify360**—Social Media information dashboards; Social Media filtering; conversion of complaints in Social Media communities to unique cases on an integrated Social CRM system.

- **Visible Technologies**—Social Media community monitoring and filtering; customizable Social Media content dashboards; content segmentation; multilanguage capabilities.

- **Buzzient**—Social Media community monitoring; exports filtered Social Media community content to Oracle-Siebel and Salesforce.com.

- **Sprout Social**—Social Media community monitoring; Social Media analytic reports; integration with Salesforce.com.

- **Sysomos**—Metrics measurement (amount and sentiment of activity); customizable dashboard; key influencers; geographic and demographic analysis.

- **Beevolve**—Social Media community monitoring; sentiment analysis; geographic and demographic analysis.

- **PeopleBrowsr**—Social Media community monitoring; demographic and sentiment analysis; interest graph; degrees of separation.

- **Social Mention**—Tracks and measures more than 100 Social Media communities; similar to Google news alerts; no analytics.

In addition, here are some free tools to check out:

- TweetDeck
- Wildfire Social Media Monitor (for Social Media campaigns)
- Hootsuite

# C

# Leading Social CRM Software Solutions

Two distinct software vendor camps are competing for Social CRM business (see Chapter 18, "Social CRM Technology Issues"). One camp is the leading Social Media platform vendors, including Lithium, INgage Networks, Mzinga, Jive, Bazaarvoice, Acquia, Moxie Software, Zimbra, and Get Satisfaction. These vendors developed the Social Media platform tools used to create Social Media communities. Their platform tools offer functionality such as blogs, discussion forums, contests, polls, user-generated content management, community tracking, and more. Around 2008, these vendors concluded that their standalone Social Media community offerings, which at the time were not tightly integrated with CRM functions, such as the customer profile, had a limited runway for growth. Consequently, these vendors—with varying degrees of success—have been expanding their Social Media platforms to include CRM functionality and linkages into CRM functionality in the areas of sales, marketing, and customer service.

In the other camp are CRM vendors that have made a major push into Social CRM over the past five or so years. These vendors include Aptean, Oracle, SAP, Infor, Salesforce.com, and update software AG. They realized that with the explosive growth in Social Media and the increased value of social insight for managing customer relationships, they needed to integrate with or create their own Social Media functionality (social monitoring, filtering, integration with Social Media platforms, and so on).

## Platform Vendors

Lithium offers a product focused on Social CRM with a goal of "one social platform" for its users. The Lithium Social Customer Experience Platform is intended to provide a single, integrated set of tools for engaging social customers in Social Media communities and on mobile devices.

This platform can facilitate the crowdsourcing of user-generated content, access gamification and search engine optimization features, and analyze the Social Media community information as a means of improving the performance of an organization's Social Media–related programs.

INgage Networks offers an application that enables organizations to create many forms of engagement through a brand community via conversations facilitated through blogs, wikis, forums, online chat, and messaging. INgage additionally offers collaboration software to facilitate the exchange of knowledge and peer-to-peer reviews with ratings and rankings (reputation system), member profiles, tagging, and search.

Mzinga offers platforms and services enabling businesses to leverage the power of Social Media such as the OmniSocial Engaged platform and the OmniSocial Learning platform for functionality in the social marketing and customer support spaces. Within its own platforms, Mzinga offers a range of moderation, listening, and social-analytics controls that are critical to the ongoing management and growth of the Social Media communities. Administrators and community managers can listen for certain watch words, see the most frequently searched terms, view which applications and topics are the most popular, and see which members are the most engaged and influential. Mzinga offers moderation services that can take place within its own platform; a competitor's platform; or any external social network such as Facebook, Twitter, YouTube, Instagram, and so on. For instance, Mzinga moderates on its OmniSocial Engaged platform for Interval International's Social Media community, where customers can discuss their travel experience and the timeshare ownership process. Mzinga moderation provides customer support and escalation in this community. Additionally, Mzinga moderates for other brands not using its platform. For instance, for Fox Broadcasting Company, Mzinga provides moderation services on its public Facebook pages and provides first-level customer support for its Fan Rewards program. Mzinga has additionally integrated with Salesforce.com so that the registered Mzinga community members' information, learning activity, and social activity can be automatically imported into an organization's Salesforce.com application. The imported information will supplement the client's existing Social CRM information with important data concerning how these individuals are interacting within the Mzinga social communities.

Jive offers a platform for communications in a Social CRM setting. The Jive platform can integrate the functionality of online communities, blogs and microblogs, discussion forums, wikis, and IM under one unified user interface. Content placed into any of the systems (blog, wiki, documentation, and so on) can be found through a common search interface.

Bazaarvoice is renowned for its ratings and reviews platform, which has been implemented by many major brands with large product catalogs. Bazaarvoice is working on its vision of the Bazaarvoice Shopper Network, which will connect up to 400 million monthly customers to create and share feedback on millions of products on a single social network.

Acquia provides a free open-source platform that offers software development kits, APIs, and other modules for a marketer to customize a Social Media community or the social elements for a website.

Moxie Software offers the Space by Moxie Social Media community software platform for employees. The Employee Engagement Spaces platform creates a business Social Media community to connect internal employees and with business partners for collaboration on a global basis.

Zimbra's community platform is designed to support external public- and private-facing communities for digital marketing, customer support, and networking. The platform can support various media formats, customizable search options, and advanced mobile features. Zimbra also offers a large ecosystem, including the Widget Studio and the Zimbra Marketplace (a virtual exchange for Zimbra application partners to market accessible applications that add value to the community customers on the Zimbra community platform). For the export of relevant Social Media community information, Zimbra has completed integrations for its customers with the Salesforce.com, Oracle Siebel, and Microsoft Dynamics CRM applications (via REST-based web services or other APIs). These Zimbra customers have moved the relevant Social Media content into their Social CRM system and afterward used their business-analytics applications to rigorously analyze the Social Media content as a means of assisting management with its business decision-making processes. Subsequently, these Zimbra customers fed their analysis of relevant Social Media information back into their Zimbra communities for use in their sales, marketing, and customer service endeavors.

Get Satisfaction offers a customer community software platform for technical support and customer service. Organizations can respond to issues regarding their products or services. All official responses are marked as such to separate them from community members' responses. Users can rate the responses based on how well they resolve the issue. The Get Satisfaction platform is well regarded for its search engine optimization, gamification, and advanced mobile features.

All of these companies have moved from C2C to B2C and B2B markets and are offering the linkage from Social Media to Social CRM.

## CRM Vendors

Meanwhile, key CRM vendors such as Aptean, Oracle, and SAP now offer a separate software module within their CRM suite that can integrate with Facebook, Twitter, LinkedIn, Google+, and other Social Media communities. Users of these three CRM applications can find out what their contacts are talking about on Facebook, Twitter, LinkedIn, Google+, and other Social Media communities, while searching for discussions within these Social Media communities on specific topics, all as a means to create new leads, service tickets, or sales-oriented actions. In the Aptean, Oracle, and SAP CRM applications, users can furthermore store and track relevant information concerning a contact posted within various Social Media communities for use in future sales activities, marketing campaigns, and for customer service.

Infor offers the Infor Social Commerce Advisor application, which can bring social data enrichment for a customer profile. With this application, Infor's clients can bring in social profile attributes (sentiment, number of Facebook friends/Twitter followers, number of posts per week/month/year, and so on) into the appropriate customer profiles within their Infor Social CRM system. Bringing in social profile attributes provides a new methodology for the marketing staff toward creating new marketing segmentations and conducting new marketing campaigns.

Infor currently leverages the Social Media monitoring tools available in the marketplace. Infor has a partnership with AwarenessHub (a Social Media platform that allows marketers to publish, manage, measure, and engage with multiple Social Media communities). However, Infor is agnostic to the Social Media monitoring platform being used (for example, Radian6, AwarenessHub, Attensity, Visible Technologies, Buzzient, and Sprout Social) as long as the Infor user can access the desired Social Media information to determine the desired Social Media metrics from a usability perspective.

Within Infor, the first clean filtering phase is completed via the Social Media monitoring tools. The second clean filtering phase is completed when the data is pulled into the Infor system. Data can be exported from Social Media communities into the Infor system via an ETL process, which provides for the de-duplication of data and the routing of the Social Media data into the appropriate customer profile.

Salesforce.com is integrating its purchased Jigsaw application (an online business directory of companies and business professionals that is built, maintained, and accessed by a worldwide community) into its main application and is offering Chatter (a Facebook-like setting for an internal organizational Social Media communications platform) as part of its attempt to make its application as easy to use as Facebook or Twitter. Jigsaw is being used to access and qualify leads and opportunities. It is also being integrated into Chatter. Salesforce.com's approach is to create a collaboration platform and integrate Social Media functions such as Jigsaw into the platform.

Salesforce.com also has a Service Cloud application that can capture tweets or comments from Facebook, bringing the content into Salesforce.com's knowledgebase to make it available for Google searches. People can conduct a Google search and go directly to Salesforce.com to get information or go directly to Facebook to get the same information, thereby closing a crucial loop in the integration of Social CRM and Social Media. Salesforce.com currently owns Radian6 and is integrating its Social Media community monitoring/filtering functionality into the Salesforce.com application.

Update software AG provides a COSMIC (Comprehensive Observation of Social Media Integrated with CRM) module within its Social CRM application, with a built-in analytic engine to determine the sentiment of the posts (for example, positive, neutral, and negative) in Facebook, Twitter, YouTube, and other Social Media communities based on keyword algorithms. Social Media community posts can be saved to a contact, account, and opportunity profile within the update Social CRM application. Each Social Media community post can be saved with a sentimentality and relevancy score. The update Social CRM application additionally provides search functionality for saved Social Media community posts by criteria such as keyword, sentimentality, relevancy, and source. Users furthermore have the ability to view the sentimentality trend of comments posted within various Social Media communities over a specific time period on a "sentiment evolution" chart.

At present, every one of the leading vendors would like to carve out a solution based on their approach to Social Media. However, with the constant change going on in Social Media today, it is difficult to lock into an approach that will completely dominate the Social Media marketplace. A closer look at the Social Media vendors mentioned previously in this chapter reveals how much they have changed in the past two years. With all of the confusion, there is no decisive leader in the Social

Media marketplace, but by examining the growth of Facebook, Twitter, and LinkedIn, it is clear that all of the leading vendors are trying to make Social Media functionality simpler to incorporate and use in a variety of different B2B or B2C business settings.

# D

# Social CRM Technology Trends

Staying on top of Social CRM technology trends (see Chapter 19, "Customers of the Future and Their Impact on Social CRM") has become increasingly difficult because of the proliferation of Social CRM technologies offered in the marketplace. Rather than trying to keep up with each new technology, organizations should track major technology developments that are most likely to impact the Social CRM industry's future, as well as their own organizational Social CRM efforts.

Here are seven major technology trends impacting the technical evolution of Social CRM that should be considered when selecting a Social CRM application:

- Client/server architecture enhancements
- XML playing a major role in Social CRM
- Social CRM vendors including more portal architecture
- Growing options for filtering/exporting relevant Social Media community information
- Social CRM vendors incorporating Business Intelligence
- Social CRM vendors associating themselves with ROA
- Growing options in licensing/hosting Social CRM

## Client/Server Architecture Enhancements

Over the last few years, technologists that have helped to drive the growth of the Web have created new architectures to accommodate increased Internet traffic and other demands. Some Social CRM vendors have embraced N-tiered, web-centric, and XML-enabled technologies. These vendors have moved away from the client/server with a three-tiered architecture to one with an N-tiered architecture.

Client/server architectures permit the two-way transfer of selected new or modified data. This data will be continually updated as the changed data is transferred between the clients and the server. Connectivity can be set with existing databases, regardless of their location, platform, or data format. This allows an organization to maintain their current information technology investments. Although some Social CRM vendors offer client/server architecture, the industry is in the middle of a major change in architectures with the growing appeal of SaaS/Cloud options. However, given some challenges relating to data ownership in SaaS/Cloud applications, the industry is likely to see some form of the client/server architecture continue to be prevalent for some time to come.

Some software vendors have adopted 100-percent web-centric architectures. Other vendors still have both products (client/server and SaaS/Cloud) and have forced customers to develop in two different architectures; this raises the costs for both systems integration and customization. For this reason, you should perform a thorough analysis and understand the vendor's architectures before leaping into a new Social CRM architecture.

## XML Playing a Major Role

Leading Social CRM vendors have not hesitated to add XML functionality to their platforms to achieve Social CRM functionality. XML is flexible because it provides a data standard that can encode the content, semantics, and schemata for a variety of cases. The functionality can be as simple as a document definition or as complex as a standalone applet that operates in a disconnected mode. Here are some examples of where XML can be used in Social CRM:

- A structured record, such as a customer record. The XML architecture allows such an item to be contained as an individual object.
- An object with data and methods, such as the persistent form of a Java object or ActiveX control. This permits even more information on customers and their Social Media history to be contained.
- A data record, such as the result set of a query, can be saved and viewed at a later time or distributed. Data warehouses can store this type of XML data.

- A standard schema entity and type. This allows for a standardized format for items such as client records, Social Media messages, and so on.

## Portal Architecture

Portals in the form of Social CRM dashboards provide a way to put a customized face onto an organization's Social CRM application. Several Social CRM vendors are beginning to personalize Social CRM portals to attractively display key Social Media analytics and/or statistics.

Personalization, within a portal environment, can come in many different flavors for key Social CRM analytics and/or statistics:

- Customer personalization
- Partner hub personalization
- Sales rep personalization
- Management personalization
- Employee personalization

Whatever the organization's requirements, rest assured that more vendors will offer some of these portal features in the future. Many vendors also have the flexibility to customize portals because they chose to develop them with enterprise software vendor frameworks and use application server engines via application service vendors.

Here are some examples of Social CRM dashboard offered by key Social CRM vendors:

- **Infor CRM** offers operational and marketing dashboard/portals to display key Social Media analytics and/or statistics. Users can customize the metrics they want to see and follow (lists, numerical values, and so on), along with graphical displays (pie charts, bar charts, line charts, and so on).
- **Update CRM** offers users the ability, via the customization of iFrames, to integrate external blogs and forums within the update CRM application for easy-access personal user dashboards. Users can also customize a Social Media dashboard with Social Media–related metrics.

- **SAP CRM** offers users the ability to access the Service Dashboard, which indicates the degree of sentiment towards a topic on Twitter (for example, positive, neutral, or negative) via integration with the SAP Twitter Customer Service application.

- **Salesforce.com** provides users with the ability to set and monitor statistics from Chatter in the Sales Tool Usage Dashboard. Users can also access a Social Media–related dashboard (number of posts, tweets from a Twitter account, and so on) via integration with the Salesforce.com Radian6 application.

- **Aptean's Pivotal CRM** provides users with the ability to access a Social Media dashboard with charts showing the number of leads, support incidents, and tasks created from Social Media status updates, as well as the status of the incidents/tasks created from the Social Media status updates.

# Growing Options for Filtering/Exporting Relevant Social Media/Community

## *Information*

Because Social Media is currently a young marketplace, there is no prevalent standard method of filtering relevant information within Social Media communities and bringing this "social insight" information into the appropriate place within a Social CRM system. Rather, I have found that Social Media vendors use multiple methods for the filtering and exporting of relevant social insight. Here are the most current common methods of filtering and exporting social insight into a Social CRM system:

- **JavaScript**—Most Social Media solutions use some form of Java-Script to monitor, filter, and export relevant Social Media data into the appropriate places within a Social CRM system. JavaScript can run locally in a user's browser (rather than on a remote server), and the browser can respond to user actions, thus quickly making an application more responsive.

- **Apache Solr Search**—Apache Solr is a highly scalable open-source search platform that is popular on websites because it can index and search multiple sites. Solr's major features include full-text search, keyword highlighting, faceted search, dynamic clustering, and database integration. The external configuration of Solr enables it to be tailored to many types of applications without Java coding, and it has a plug-in architecture to support advanced customization. Solr can furthermore return recommendations for related content based on the search query. Solr offers APIs for JavaScript object notification and the Python and Ruby programming languages.

- **RSS (XML)**—Really Simple Syndication uses a family of standard web feed formats to send and publish frequently updated information. The RSS feeds enable publishers to syndicate data automatically. A standard XML file format ensures compatibility with many different programs. The RSS feeds benefit users who want to receive timely and regular updates from their favorite Social Media communities. With an RSS subscription, the user's browser will continuously monitor a Social Media community and inform the user of any updates. The browser can also be set to automatically download/export any new data of interest to be placed in the appropriate place within a Social CRM system, which can be set up via Representational State Transfer (REST) based endpoints. REST is an architecture style for designing networked applications and uses simple HTTP requests to read and post data between machines (I will discuss REST further in the Resource Oriented Architecture trend.).

The most applicable method for filtering and exporting relevant Social Media information into a Social CRM system will differ depending on each individual organization's needs and budget. I would recommend that the executives of each organization initiating a Social CRM initiative discuss the technical and economic feasibility of each potential filtering/exporting methodology with the organization's IT department to determine which methodology would be the most appropriate. Because the Social CRM market is still in an early stage of growth, I expect there will be additional options for filtering/exporting relevant Social Media information into CRM systems within the near future.

## Business Intelligence

Analytic applications vendors are quickly merging with customer intelligence and Social CRM providers. If organizations are not privy to changes in their corporate landscape, they are more likely to be blindsided. The convergence of the BI (Business Intelligence) and Social Media communities is the critical next step in supplying organizational infrastructures with the decision-making capabilities and web-enabled functions they need to move forward in Social CRM. From a BI standpoint, organizations leverage their Social CRM investment by pulling information from their Social CRM system into a separate, organized intelligent structure where educated analysis and decisions can be made. This information helps them leverage their Social Media communities with their existing data warehouse to create the overall infrastructure needed to support and supply BI information for their Social CRM initiatives.

Organizations must also continually gather information about their competitors to stay on top of their game. Social CRM applications are able to consistently collect competitive information from Social Media communities and store it in a data warehouse or within the appropriate place in the Social CRM system for analysis.

The new BI analytic applications provide the following four key capabilities:

- The ability to quantify the value of the Social CRM information
- The ability to set thresholds to trigger rules and events (automating the delivery of specific content such as personalized offers and product recommendations based on Social CRM–related criteria, such as keywords, sentiment value, and so on)
- The ability to help qualify Social CRM information
- The ability to evaluate Social CRM–related business processes and their effectiveness.

A *data warehouse* is a large analytical database that can serve as the foundation for BI activities. Data warehousing is a process supported by several underlying enabling technologies such as data extraction, transformation, and load (ETL) tools. The underlying framework is the data store that is built on popular database engines, including Microsoft SQL Server and Oracle, that support online analytical processing (OLAP) technology. The data extraction on the surface uses ETL software. Some of the current ETL software includes IBM Cognos, Information Builders, and Informatica. In some cases, data warehouses utilize ROLAP or MOLAP (cubes) technology. Some companies have pre-built ETL templates for popular ETL tools to automatically create an out-of-the-box data warehouse and set of reports for immediate BI use. An example would be the Oracle Business Intelligence offering.

*Data mining* can best be described as a BI technology that has various techniques to extract comprehensible, hidden, and useful information from a data population. Data mining makes it possible to discover hidden trends and patterns in large amounts of data. The current technology for this is data analyzers, which can be integrated with a Social CRM suite such as Oracle's Performance Analyzer that generates data and makes it available to a Social CRM application. Data analyzer packages can also be integrated into the SAP and Salesforce.com Social CRM products via the SAP Netweaver and Salesforce.com AppExchange applications, respectively. The new data analyzer technology can provide an organization with predictive analytic functionality, which enables their employees to determine current consumer trends and make decisions based on competitive insights and correlated data.

BI functionality deals with a lower complexity methodology (such as ad hoc querying/reporting, data-mining techniques, structured data, typical sources, and small to mid-size data sets) than predictive analytics/data mining. With the advent of Big Data analytics and insight, the market is entering into a degree of higher business value and higher complexity in terms of what is available both from a data and analytics perspective. We can now conduct optimizations and predictive analytics/data mining using sophisticated algorithms with all sorts of data types and large data sets. Additionally, much more analysis is being done in real time, such as real-time decisioning (for example, Amazon's individualized purchase recommendations based on a person's own prior purchases and other customers purchasing similar products). The real-time decisioning process is a harboring of how many organizations will conduct their business in the near future. For more information on implications of Big Data, turn to Chapter 22, "The Impact of Big Data Analytics and Insight on Social CRM."

## Resource Oriented Architecture

There is a recent trend in the Social CRM marketplace of moving away from SOAP-based Service Oriented Architecture (SOA) toward more direct RESTful-style web resources and consequently Resource Oriented Architecture (ROA). ROA is a style of software architecture and programming paradigm for designing and developing software in the form of resources with RESTful interfaces. These resources are software components (discrete pieces of code and/or data structures) that can be reused for different purposes.

ROA design principles and guidelines are used during the phases of software development and system integration. ROA is associated closely with the Web and is useful for businesses that use the Web as the computing/publishing platform of choice; it is therefore potentially very attractive to Social CRM vendors. Because ROA only uses the well-known basic technologies of the Web, it is much easier to use than the SOAP-based SOA approach (based on services), which has its own unique and extensive technology stack.

ROA is typically used in open systems, which is conducive to Social CRM success in the export of relevant Social Media information. As mentioned previously, in ROA architectures there typically would be RESTful services. RESTful services are now often implemented with XML over HTTP. The main advantage of REST is its ease of implementation, the agility of its design, and its lightweight approach to complex mechanisms in comparison to the SOAP-based SOA. Other advantages of REST lie with its performance: With better cache support, lightweight requests/responses, and easier response analysis, REST allows for nimbler clients and servers and reduces network traffic.

## Growing Options in Licensing/Hosting Social CRM

As the Social CRM market matures, more flexible licensing options have become available for Social CRM software applications. Old licensing models continue to exist, such as licenses by user and concurrency, but these new licensing models add options for organizations to choose from.

Here are two major licensing options for Social CRM software applications:

- **Subscription licensing**—An organization subscribes to the Social CRM application, and it is accessed via the Internet using a SaaS/Cloud application. Some Social Media vendor platforms, such as Mzinga, Zimbra, and Lithium, are now offered on a subscription license similar to the subscription licensing option offered by Salesforce.com.

- **Perpetual licensing**—The organization owns the Social CRM application, but it resides at a service provider's data center or on the premises. Some Social Media platform and Social CRM vendor applications such as Zimbra, Pivotal CRM, and Infor can provide their software via the perpetual licensing option.

Many Social CRM software vendor applications are being offered in the form of a SaaS/Cloud application. SaaS (Software as a Service) typically is a multitenant application that uses an outsourced framework service to build an application over the Web. In the past, it was possible to outsource within a mainframe Customer Information Control System (CICS) environment, but applications still needed to be developed with coding. In today's marketplace, it is technically feasible to build a fairly robust application with little or no coding. Examples of SaaS Social CRM vendors include Lithium, Mzinga, and Salesforce.com, which provide common business applications online that are accessed from a browser, while the software and data are stored on the SaaS/Cloud servers.

Many analysts expect SaaS/Cloud offerings to become the dominant form of delivery for years to come. According to Tim Bajarin of Creative Strategies:[1]

> "Now we have giant data centers in multiple places, we have structured data and information in the Cloud. This is the heart of next generation computing. This is ironic for those of us who have gone from the mainframe to mini-computers. It really frees up our personal terminal to become much more of a personal tool. It has an impact on the way applications will be developed and how people will use them in the future."

Although some customers prefer the convenience of the SaaS/Cloud option, other customers, such as banks, large technology companies, and government agencies, still prefer the on-premises option. It provides them with complete control of their Social Media community data, ensuring that they can run their communities within their own data center, as well as control the integration/analysis of their own Social Media community data with other internal and external applications.

# Endnotes

1. destinationCRM 2008 Conference, August 2008

# E

# Addressing Social CRM Security Risks

As noted in Chapter 20, "The Impact of Mobility on Social CRM," the growth of Social CRM is exposing organizations to more risk than ever before. Social Media communities open the organization to all kinds of new exposure. What's more, additional risk comes from other components of Social CRM technology, including hardware, software, operating systems, middleware, and networks. Minimizing security risk for Social CRM is similar to other applications that leverage the Internet: The organization needs to create a security culture and then provide the tools to reduce security risks. Robert Richardson, the former Director of the Computer Security Institute, stated in the Computer Security Institute's Computer Crime and Security Annual Survey:

> "Information security is a complex undertaking, but it is also an essential one in the current, highly-networked world. Organizations that hope to thrive have to create a culture that willingly funds, trains, and empowers an enterprise information security function, because attacks happen with regularity and their impact can be significant."

In the Computer Security Institute's Computer Crime and Security Survey, the following range of attacks and abuses were noted by respondents:

- Fifty-nine percent detected employee abuse of Internet access privileges (for example, downloading pirated software and inappropriate use of email systems).
- Fifty-two percent detected computer viruses.
- Fifty percent reported losses from laptop or mobile device theft.
- Twenty-six percent of respondents detected phishing where their organization was fraudulently represented as the sender of an email.
- Twenty-five percent detected denial-of-service attacks.

Given the important Social CRM component of monitoring Social Media communities over the Internet, to prevent Social CRM–related security problems, the organization must at a minimum address network infrastructure risks. A best practice to address risk is to create a written information security policy that establishes what must be done to protect information stored on all computer and mobile devices. It should contain a sufficient definition of "what" to do so that the "how" can be identified and measured or evaluated.

## Areas Addressed by a Security Policy

A well-written information security policy addresses these types of risks:

- **Remote access**
  - Laptops (for example, viruses, password protection, applications and operating systems, encryption, personal firewalls, encryption devices, token management, enterprise firewalls, and data backup)
  - Handheld devices, including tablets (for example, password protection, virus protection, enterprise firewalls, encryption, and potentially wireless encryption)
  - Virtual private networks, or VPNs (for example, enterprise firewalls and network-provider password management)
  - Remote Access Service (for example, RAS server passwords and enterprise firewalls)
  - Application-level security, including Social Media and Social CRM (for example, workgroup, user, and field level)

- **Ebusiness/ecommerce (for customer engagement)**
  - Social CRM, portal, web self-service, and ebusiness application security (for example, user and field level)
  - Public Key Infrastructure (PKI)
  - VPNs and web services

- **Call center email (for customer engagement)**
  - Virus protection
  - Help desk access

- **Enterprise email (for customer engagement)**
  - User list management
  - Lightweight Directory Access Protocol, or LDAP (used for email user management)
  - Password management
  - Server email attachment virus protection
  - Web access management

- **Enterprise security**
  - Intrusion detection
  - LDAP (used in firewalls, segmentation, authentication, and email user-management authorization)
  - Wireless protocol
  - Password management
  - Network operating system password management
  - Virus protection
  - Demilitarized zones (DMZs)
  - Firewalls (external and office-to-office) and network, proxy, and packet filter gateways
  - Internet access (surf control)

Although not all security holes can be plugged, organizations should strive to define an acceptable level of risk at a reasonable cost. Identifying the threats or risks that an enterprise may face will help in identifying the vulnerabilities and will assist in selecting the appropriate security measures for protection. Management today must learn the new industry terminology, and proactively become aware of the security issues. Prior to the setting of security policy, the following are critical trends and areas where more education is needed.

## The Human Factor

People in the organization are the weakest link. Everyone in the organization, from the customer service representative in the contact center to the sales executives equipped with wireless-enabled laptops, can inadvertently—or intentionally—create a security breach. One aspect of human behavior is a given: If you try hard enough, you can find someone who will believe nearly anything. Hackers (people outside the organization who inflict chaos) know this and often create plausible stories to entice information from an organization's employees. Unwittingly, an organization's employees can open the door to these attacks, often innocently (for example, by simply passing an email along). The malicious employee is the individual who intentionally inflicts damage to the network. This type of damage can consist of anything from releasing a virus, stealing information, and poisoning data, to bypassing security controls to play games on the organization's dime. All statistics show that millions of dollars are lost each year as a result of employee security breaches.

The Internet provides hackers with potential access from anywhere in the world. Some of these people are looking for some sort of intellectual high, whereas others are fueled by more treacherous motives, such as revenge or stealing for profit. In any event, no intrusion is innocent, and no intrusion is benign.

The other people issue involves the difficulty in attracting and keeping skilled employees. The lack of skilled employees leads to another common threat, which can be as simple as the misconfiguration of servers and firewalls from the manufacturer or even an organization's network from the inside. Educating employees is key, and this includes educating the people involved with setting the policy and making the system secure. The threats to a Social CRM system can come in many forms: disgruntled employees, corporate espionage, lax system administrators, faulty products, and poorly educated users.

### Systems and Software

Other risks to the Social CRM enterprise reside on employees' PCs, laptops, tablets, and other handheld devices. Malicious code (sometimes called *malware*) can take different forms: a computer virus, a Trojan horse (a program that purports to do one thing, but creates a security vulnerability), and even active content such as Java and ActiveX programs. Other harmful agents are worms, such as Nimda and Duqu, which can distribute themselves without the help of people. The good news is that excellent antivirus protection tools exist, and the latest versions should be implemented by the organization; however, they must be coupled with prudent end-user behavior to be effective. The immediate need is to secure the network where the organization's devices communicate. Organizations must look at organizational firewalls and even personal firewalls for employees with home-based PCs, laptops, tablets, and other handheld devices that connect via a cable modem, DSL, or Wi-Fi.

Software vendors purposely try to make installing software easy. Even if the user knows nothing about software, they can select the system defaults in the software installation program. To reduce the number of attack points, employees should turn off any software functionality that they do not plan to use (this may require assistance from the IT department). Internet firewalls are only as good as their configuration. Eliminating risk through this method is known as *hardening* and offers fewer entry points into the network. Because networks are in a constant state of change due to upgrades and add-ons, constant adjustments are being made to the software settings. This only adds to the frustration of assuming that the settings for a particular software installation are secure. It is almost impossible to prevent new security holes from appearing as software updates take place.

The complexity of software combinations makes it practically impossible to evaluate the overall systems software in sufficient detail to discover and resolve all potential security exposures. In some cases, users count on each software component being well designed from a security standpoint and strive to minimize exposures resulting from combining and integrating the software. Many times, system administrators must take it on faith that the components will enforce acceptable security.

How do organizations judge the risks embedded in their current Social CRM systems? How do they determine if the investments related to reducing risks are warranted? The essential elements of risk and cost involve the following:

- What resources need to be protected?
- What is the cost of loss or compromise?
- What is the cost of protection?
- What is the likelihood of loss or compromise?
- What is the cost to the organization?

The IT manager has no proven mechanisms to compute the organization's vulnerability because the effectiveness of security countermeasures defies quantification. Unfortunately, in the real world, organizations face budgetary constraints, so security choices have to be made. What is the probability of a security breach versus the expense? IT managers can develop metrics that may not be foolproof but still allow for guidelines as they evaluate the cost of security measures. The following table is fictitious, but it could be a guideline for developing a way of answering the previous questions:

| Countermeasure | Cost of Compromise | Cost of Protection | Probability of Compromise |
|---|---|---|---|
| Install firewall | $1,000,000 | $25,000 | 50 percent |
| Audit analog lines | $50,000 | $2,000 | 5 percent |
| Develop security policy | $1,000,000 | $40,000 | 75 percent |

The organization needs to decide which risks should receive what level of attention and investment. These decisions must be documented and must guide all implementation plans for Social CRM applications. They must also be aligned with the organization's agreed-on security policy.

According to industry estimates, security policy budgets should be set to about 5 percent of the organization's IT budget. Unfortunately, security budgets are too often embedded in individual projects, which increases the cost of each project. A dedicated budget that's established to address identified risks should be allocated and reconciled with individual business unit budgets.

# Developing the Security Policy

First, securing a network can ensure the following goals:

- Confidentiality
- Integrity
- Availability

Because no one technology or process can be implemented in the name of total security, the aim is to develop a defense through an in-depth strategy. Start with important security principles and corporate security standards. Use the following guidelines in this development:

- Appoint a high-level executive with organization-wide responsibilities to enforce and develop security policies consistently across the organization.
- Ensure that security policies are holistically defined and enforced across the Social CRM environment, from applications to networks

to physical servers, laptops, and handheld devices. Because the IT systems belong to the organization, they are designed to further the interests of the organization. Enforcing the policy is essential. Organizations must hold specific individuals accountable for incidents as well as hold managers accountable for risk and budget decisions.

- Make sure the lines of business are actively involved and support the Social CRM security strategy. Because line-of-business executives can influence the majority of Social CRM funding decisions in many organizations, not having their buy-in can lead to the loss of productivity gains from corporate security investments, as the business units continue to "reinvent" security within their applications in an inconsistent and unpredictable manner. The key to success is not only the dos and don'ts but also providing a sense of the whys.

- Think and plan ahead. Think at least six to 12 months ahead while giving the lines of business the tools needed to build the secure Social CRM environment without creating a security infrastructure that will become yet another legacy infrastructure within a few months.

- Understand the links between Social CRM security and customer satisfaction. In many businesses, customer intimacy, loyalty, and satisfaction are imperative. A complex security infrastructure, despite its security-oriented benefits, may impede customer satisfaction. Enforcing policies such as password guidelines that ensure single sign-on can bring the complexity of security under control to help increase customer satisfaction. It is not abnormal to find organizations that require employees, customers, and partners to input multiple passwords within one application. This is a nonstarter for users of Social Media communities.

- Create a single, well-known focal point for security incident reporting. Even with intrusion detection in place, break-ins will occur, but any hope of containment needs to be acted on quickly. All users can assist with this effort, but a well-designed system will facilitate containment.

- Enforce good administration practices. Control administration consistently from a central policy, but allow flexibility to delegate certain administrative security tasks to business units, partners, or others based on the needs of the growing business. All security policies and procedures should be clearly outlined with consistent follow-up; simultaneously, enforcement needs to become part of the organizational culture.

- Develop authentication rules. The most common method is to use passwords for user access, but alternatives include the use of security tokens and encryption. Make sure password rules are spelled out and enforced.

- Social CRM security should provide abstract, job, data, and duty roles that work together to control access to functions and data. This role-based access control (RBAC) should normalize access to functions and data through user roles rather than only users. User access should be based on the definition of the roles provisioned to the user. The RBAC will secure access in a "Who can do what on which functions or sets of data under what conditions" approach.

- Implement active content screening tools (virus protection) and have rules for downloading from Internet sites and email attachments.

- Use open standards. Using multivendor, open standards in vendor selection and product choice is a key requirement to current and future flexibility and interoperability.

- Beware of any vendor who promises a complete security solution with only its product portfolio. Strong business partnerships are critical in end-to-end security control.

- Don't stop updating the policy and checking security. Review the organization's information protection or information security programs. Get assistance, call on experts, and use available tools. For example, Microsoft offers a free tool, the Microsoft Baseline Security Analyzer, which is designed to help organizations assess security weaknesses in the current IT security environment and provide specific guidance to minimize these weaknesses.

- Ensure that data is backed up frequently. A good policy might include which systems need to be backed up, how often, who will perform the backups, and so on. This can be incorporated into a disaster recovery policy that provides for quick recovery from any loss. Create a contingency plan that covers all possible scenarios that would result in a loss of data and property.

- And, finally, educate, educate, educate. Annual or semiannual security training for end users and administrators is a must. To maintain a strong security posture, members of an organization should know what to look for concerning security risks. Knowing how to report problems or incidents is also critical in maintaining that posture. Make sure administrators are educated on current technology and can adequately secure the organization's Social CRM system.

The ability to deliver computer security and information privacy assurance is critical to the future of Social CRM. Even though the technology community offers new solutions to security problems, IT managers must put this technology through a systematic risk-management process. Although most organizations do not yet handle the process for managing security well, a focused effort can lead to notable improvement. This focus includes analyzing risks, setting a specific security budget, and, of course, creating a security policy. Remember that Social CRM security is critical for the success of the Social CRM system.

# A Glossary of Terms

**Apache Solr**—A highly scalable open-source search platform that is popular for websites because it can index and search multiple sites.

**Beacon**—A very small transmitting radio that sends relevant information to a desired location.

**Big Data**—Data-driven, tactical decision-making derived from large data volumes coming from a variety of sources (for example, transactional, Social Media, mobile devices, electronic transactions, and others).

**Blog**—A discussion or informational website published on the Internet and consisting of discrete entries typically displayed in reverse chronological order and generally archived on a periodic basis. Blogs are mostly used to express opinions on topical events such as sports, music, fashion, or politics, but in the past years, they have emerged as established communication channels for businesses as well as individuals.

**Bluetooth Low Energy Technology**—A wireless technology standard for exchanging data efficiently over short distances from fixed and mobile devices.

**Business Intelligence**—The transformation of raw data into meaningful and useful information for business-analysis purposes.

**Channel/Partner Collaboration**—A two-way dialog with an organization's channel members and partners held within a Social Media community. This includes sharing and qualifying priority sales leads, developing customer-facing collateral, executing Go-To-Market strategies, and capturing the voice of the partner.

**Channel Optimization**—The right balance between fulfilling each customer's desired channel preferences versus achieving the organization's desire to secure the lowest cost-to-serve channel option for each customer, along with optimizing each selected channel through the use of integrated processes and technology.

**Client/Server Model**—A distributed application structure that partitions tasks or workloads between the providers of a resource or service, called *servers,* and service requesters, called *clients.* Often, clients and servers communicate over a computer network on separate hardware, but both may reside in the same system.

**Cloud Computing**—The delivery of computer services in which shared resources, software, and information are provided to computers and other devices over a network (typically the Internet).

**Customer Engagement**—The process by which the organization leverages the social insight stored in the customer profile and elsewhere within the CRM application to engage with customers or prospects via their preferred channel(s). Customer engagement provides opportunities for organizations and customers/prospects to learn from one another and to use such insight to deepen their relationships.

**Customer Intimacy**—A marketing strategy where a service supplier or product retailer gets close to its clients. The benefits of greater customer intimacy for a business might include improved highly tailored problem-solving capabilities and greater adaptation of products to customer needs, as well as higher customer loyalty levels.

**Customer Profile**—A description of a customer or set of customers that includes demographic, geographic, and psychographic characteristics such as customer information, activities, products purchased, financials, operational issues, service issues, customer insight, competitive information, marketing campaigns/opportunities, and customer news. Social Media insight can provide the emotional and sentiment characteristics of a relevant issue to a customer profile.

**Customer Relationship Management (CRM)**—A business approach that integrates people, process, and technology to maximize relationships with customers. CRM increasingly leverages the Internet and Social Media to provide seamless coordination among all customer-facing functions.

**Data Warehouse**—A central repository of integrated data from one or more disparate sources. Data warehouses store current and historical data and are used for creating trending reports for senior management, such as annual and quarterly comparisons.

**Extract, Transform, and Load (ETL)**—A process in database usage and in data warehousing that (1) extracts data from outside sources, (2) transforms it to fit operational needs, and (3) loads it into the end target (for example, a database).

**Enterprise Collaboration**—The leveraging of Social Media tools to facilitate easy sharing of information among personnel. Using a knowledge community, personnel around the globe can search for and connect to internal SMEs to address an issue. They can generate referrals and introductions leading to new potential business, and they can also collaborate and solve customer challenges by sharing what has worked elsewhere.

**Extensible Markup Language (XML)**—Markup language that defines a set of rules for encoding documents in a human-readable and machine-readable format. The design goals of XML emphasize simplicity, generality, and usability over the Internet.

**Gamification**—The use of game-like elements in non-game environments to influence behavior and the integration of game mechanics into a website, Social Media community, campaign, or application in order to drive engagement.

**Hub-and-Spoke Model**—A model in which an organization uses publically available Social Media tools such as Facebook and Twitter to drive traffic to their corporate website, which in turn is the best tool for driving traffic to their private Social Media community.

**Ideation**—The creative process of generating, developing, and communicating new ideas.

**Internet of Everything**—A global system of interconnected computer networks, sensors, actuators, and devices all using the Internet protocol. This holds so much potential to change people's lives that it is often referred to as the Internet's next generation.

**Internet of Things**—Includes any natural or manmade object that is embedded with sensors assigned an Internet address and that transfers data coming from the sensors by connecting wirelessly via the Internet to servers located in the Cloud.

**Knowledge Community**—A group of people within an enterprise who engage in knowledge-sharing activities in support of a common work interest. The knowledge community may include people from multiple disciplines within the enterprise, as well as extended-enterprise participants.

**Knowledge Management**—The discipline of enabling individuals, teams, and entire organizations to collectively and systematically create, share, and apply knowledge to better achieve their objectives.

**Microblogging**—A broadcast medium that exists in the form of blogging. A microblog differs from a traditional blog in that its content is typically smaller in both actual and aggregated file size.

**Middleware**—A separate product that serves as the connection between two applications. It is often computer software that provides services to software applications beyond those available from the operating system.

**N-tier architecture**—A client/server architecture in which, the presentation, the application processing, and the data management are logically separate processes.

**Online Analytical Processing (OLAP)**—An approach to answering multidimensional analytical queries. OLAP is part of the broader category of business intelligence, which also encompasses relational database, report writing, and data mining.

**Private Social Media Communities**—Social Media communities that are not open to everyone, but rather are targeted to customer groups with whom the organization is keen to create a two-way communication.

**Public Social Media Communities**—Social Media communities that are in theory open to everyone. Key public Social Media communities include Facebook and LinkedIn.

**Really Simple Syndication (RSS)**—A format for delivering regularly changing web content. RSS uses a family of standard web feed formats to send and publish frequently updated information.

**Representational State Transfer (REST)**—An architecture style for designing networked applications that uses simple HTTP requests to read and post data between machines.

**Resource Oriented Architecture (ROA)**—A style of software architecture and programming paradigm for designing and developing software in the form of resources with "RESTful" interfaces. ROA design principles and guidelines are used during the phases of software development and system integration.

**Software as a Service (SaaS)**—A software licensing and delivery model in which software is licensed on a subscription basis and is centrally hosted.

**Smart Devices**—Devices that have built-in, machine-to-machine communication capabilities.

**Social CRM**—The intersection of Social Media and CRM. It consists of the ability to harvest information from Social Media communities, integrate this information into customer profiles, and use the expanded profile for engagement with customers.

**Social Graph**—A graph that displays connection points between a person and other people, places, or things that a person interacts with online. The Social Graph is in essence the representation of a person's relationships online. It can thus provide for a robust analysis of Social Media data for an individual or a group of people.

**Social Insight**—Filtered Social Media community information that provides dynamic data regarding a customer or prospect's sentiment and emotional feeling about the organization that now complements the static and historical information (for example, dollars spent and history of transactions) that is typically found in a customer profile.

**Social Media**—A set of highly interactive technology tools that leverage the fundamental human desire to interact with others and provide a new way for organizations to communicate with and relate to employees, consumers, partners, and other stakeholders.

**Social Media Community**—A website that brings people with similar goals or interests together to connect and exchange information within a central location. Social Media communities offer a community culture of social rules and group dynamics that identify members. Social Media communities provide for a discussion of topics that a community or network finds mutually interesting or beneficial.

**Social Media Community Guidelines**—Rules set up in Social Media communities to ensure that the tone within the community is positive and productive for all community members.

**Social Media Community Moderation**—The moderation of all posts in a Social Media community in accordance with the community guidelines. Positive moderation rewards engagement and encourages members to participate in the community.

**Social Media Filtering**—The process of applying software applications that serve as digital crawlers that utilize rules-based filter search functionality to filter chatter in both public and private Social Media communities by criteria such as keywords, tone, sentiment, volume, demographics, location, influencer status, and more. Filtered Social Media community information can be exported to the appropriate contact profiles in a CRM system for storage and analysis.

**Social Media Monitoring/Listening**—The process of applying software applications that serve as "digital crawlers" to listen to chatter in designated Social Media communities for certain keywords, tone, sentiment, volume, demographics, location, influencer status, and more. The purpose is to track and analyze social sentiment or content regarding what customers and prospects are saying about an individual, organization, industry, brand, product, and/or service.

**Social Media Policies**—Organizational policies that inform employees what they can and cannot do when participating in Social Media communities.

**Technical Baseline Review**—The effort of the organization's technical staff to define the current technical platform and capabilities in place. This includes current hardware and software, data synchronization tools, current/planned links to Social Media communities, Social Media monitoring tools, and so on.

**Technographic Profiling**—Segmentation profiling of a customer base that focuses on the technology-related behavior of an individual.

**Wi-Fi Technology**—A local-area wireless technology that allows an electronic device to exchange data or connect to the Internet using 2.4GHz UHF and 5GHz SHF radio waves.

**Wiki**—A web application that allows people to add, modify, or delete content in collaboration with others.

# Index